I0832066

CITY POEMS.

PRINTED BY R. CLAY, LONDON,

FOR

MACMILLAN & CO. CAMBRIDGE.

London: BELL AND DALDY, 186, FLEET STREET.
Dublin: WILLIAM ROBERTSON.
Edinburgh: EDMONSTON AND DOUGLAS.
Glasgow: JAMES MACLEHOSE.
Oxford: J. H. AND JAS. PARKER.

CITY POEMS.

BY

ALEXANDER SMITH,

AUTHOR OF "A LIFE DRAMA, AND OTHER POEMS."

Cambridge:

MACMILLAN AND CO.

1857.

CONTENTS.

HORTON.

HORTON.

THE other night I lay within my bed,
Watching my dying fire: it mouldered out.
I listened to the strange nocturnal cries:
A ballad-singer 'neath my window stood,
And sang hoarse songs; she went away, and then
An oyster-man came crying through the streets;
And straight, as if I stood on dusky shores,
I saw the tremulous silver of the sea
Set to some coast beneath the mighty moon.
He passed into the silence. Wafts of song
From arm-linked youths, as they meandered home,
Came to my ears; the town grew still; and then,

Just when my soul was sinking into dream,
Alarm of "Fire!" ran through the startled street,
And windows were thrown up as it went past.
A hasty engine tore along, and trailed
A lengthening crowd behind. "Ah, ha," I thought,
"That maniac, Fire, is loose; who was so tame,
When little children looked into his face,
He laughed and blinked within his prison-grate.
His fit is on; the merry winking elf
Has rushed into a hungry crimson fiend:
Now he will seize a house, crush in the roof,
And leap and dance above his prey, and throw
His roaring flickering arms across the sky—
May he be bound again!" The tumult scared
Soft-plumaged Silence, and, when it was gone,
She settled down again with outspread wings
Upon the place she left. That angel Sleep,
Who blunts the edge of pain, who brings from Heaven
The dead ones to us, took my hand in his,
And led me down unto the under-world.

We stood beside a drowsy-creeping stream
Which ever through a land of twilight stole
Unrippled, smooth as oil. It slipped 'tween cliffs
Gloomy with pines that ne'er were vexed with wind.
The cliffs stood deep in dream. The stream slid on,
Nor murmured in its sleep. There was no noise ;
The winds were folded o'er that drowsy place ;
The poppies hung unstirred. I asked its name.
Sleep murmured "Lethe." "Drink of it," I thought,
"And all my past shall be washed out at once."
I knelt, and lifted pale beseeching hands—
"I have drunk poison, and can sleep no more ;
Give me this water, for I would forget."
But Sleep stood silent, and his eyes were closed.
"Give me this water, for I would forget ;
Give me this precious water, that I may
Bear to my brothers in the upper-world,
And they shall call me 'happy,' 'Sent of God,'
And Earth shall rest." Sleep answered, "Every night
When I am sitting 'neath the lonely stars,

The world within my lap, I hear it mourn
Like a sick child; something afflicts it sore,
I cannot give it rest." Upon these words
I hid my face awhile, then cried aloud,
"No one can give forgetfulness; not one.
No one can tell me who can give it me.
I asked of Joy, as he went laughing past,
Crushing a bunch of grapes against his lips,
And suddenly the light forsook his face,
His orbs were blind with tears—*he* could not tell.
I asked of Grief, as with red eyes he came
From a sweet infant's bier; and at the sound
He started, shook his head, with quick hand drew
His mantle o'er his face, and turned away
'Mong the blue twilight-mists." Sleep did not raise
His heavy lids, but in a drowsy voice,
Like murmur of a leafy sycamore
When bees are swarming in the glimmering leaves,
Said, "I've a younger brother, very wise,
Silent and still, who ever dwells alone—

His name is Death: seek him, and he may know."
I cried, "O angel, is there no one else?"
But Sleep stood silent, and his eyes were closed.

Methought, when I awoke, "We have two lives;
The soul of man is like the rolling world,
One half in day, the other dipt in night;
The one has music and the flying cloud,
The other, silence and the wakeful stars."
I drew my window-curtains, and instead
Of the used yesterday, there laughing stood
A new-born morning from the Infinite
Before my very face; my heart leaped up.
Inexorable Labour called me forth;
And as I hurried through the busy streets,
There was a sense of envy in my heart
Of lazy lengths of rivers in the sun,
Larks soaring up the ever-soaring sky,
And mild kine couched in fields of uncrushed dew.

With earnest faces bent above their tasks,
Some ten or twelve sat with me in the room.
He at my right hand ever dwelt alone:
A moat of dulness fenced him from the world.
My left hand neighbour was all flame and air,
A restless spirit veering like the wind:
And what a lover! what an amorous heart!
In the pure fire and fervency of love,
Leander, like the image of a star
Within the thrilling sea, was scarce his match.
His love for each new Hero of a week,
No Hellespont could cool. Among the rest,
Sat one with visage red with sun and wind
As the last hip upon the frosted brier
When the blithe huntsman snuffs the hoary morn.
He poached at night in every stream for miles;
Knew nests in every wood. Much did he love
To gather fragments of the broken past;
Swords from old fields; carvings from hollow towers
The wind inhabits; heath from martyrs' graves

Asleep in sunshine on warm summer moors;
And one rude splinter did he cherish much,
Struck from the stone that with unwearied hand
Held up the exulting banner of the Bruce,
Which all that proud day laughed with glorious scorn
Upon its baffled foes. And there was one
Who strove most valiantly to be a man,
Who smoked and still got sick, drank hard and woke
Each morn with headache; his poor timorous voice
Trembled beneath the burden of the oaths
His bold heart made it bear. He sneered at love,
Was not so weak as to believe the sex
Cumbered with virtue. O he knew! he knew!
He had himself adventured in that sea,
Could tell, Sir, if he would—yet never dared
Speak to a lady in his life without
Blushing hot to the ears. 'Mong these I sat.

The clouds flew from the east unto the west;
St. Stephen, from his airy coronet,

In music told the quarters and the hours.
We talked of all this tangled dance of Deaths,
Wild-haired and naked Pleasures, Satyrs, Drolls,
Which men call Life; of early Love, which makes
A dusty street a sunbeam, daily meals
Enchanted tables spread by angel hands,
And rough serge glistering gold; of the strange light,
The incredible bliss, summed in the word "beloved,"
When the poor heart, bewildered with its joy,
Half fears that it is fooled; this Pantomime,
In which the speckled Clown wins every trick;
Astonished Pantaloon, the kicks and jeers;
Rich Harlequin, the glittering Columbine,
Brave dress, enjoyment, universal power;
A single slap of his enchanted sword,
Grim caverns open into trees of gold—
At which, mayhap, an angel audience sits,
Mingling strange comment with its wildness. Then
We talked about the painter, him who dwelt
Within the white house on the moor, alone,

No wife to love or hate, no human bud
To burst in flower beneath his loving eye.
An empire's fall was less in his regard
Than sunshine pouring from the rifted clouds
On an old roof-tree furred with emerald moss;
A wide grey windy sea bespecked with foam,
A ship beneath bare poles against the rain;
Or thunder steeping all the sunny waste
In ominous light. One keen clear autumn day
The place was filled with silent sabled men
Standing in whispering knots. Within an hour
The empty house was left to whistling winds
In which the curlew sailed with wavering cry,
And flying sunny gleams—a dark red mound
Six paces on the moor. Nature he loved,
Death was the priest that wed them; he is hers
Henceforward now for ever. Then I heard
How Charles stood 'mid the roses in the porch;
Within, his Cousin watched the earliest star,
With white hands fluttering o'er the keys,—fair hands

By lingering music kissed! A step—she turned,
Their eyes met, and that swift flash made them one
For ever—in all worlds. A voice then told
How on a certain night, Wat, James, and John
Saw in the moonlight park three giddy girls
Mingling with their own shadows in the dance:
John gave a cry, each darted like a bird,
Leaving a wake of laughter as she flew.
Flushed with the chase, 'mid laughter-smothered shrieks,
Wat robbed a ruffled struggler of a kiss.
Poor Wat—once proud as Chanticleer that struts
Among his dames; faint challenged, claps his wings
And crows defiance to the distant farms—
Now meekly sits beneath a shrewish voice,
With children round his knee. We spoke of him
Who drew sweet Mary Hawthorne into shame:
We could remember that for many years,
With her blithe smile and gleam of golden hair,
She like a candle lit her father's hearth,
Making the old man glad.—Now long rank grass

Hides a neglected grave. Then all at once
Discourse burst from its melancholy weeds,
As brilliant as a spangled dancing-girl:
Each pelted each with quip and raillery;
And when from laughing lips a jest broke loose,
The pack of wits opened in loud pursuit,
And ran it to the death. Uprose my Dream
From its dim lair—for somehow, in my mind,
As the deserted East with mournful eyes
Stands far back, gazing on the glowing West,
Death ever looks on joy. "Ere long," I thought,
"Great Death will hallow all these flippant lips,
And make each poor face awful. Truest tears
Will not seem wasted when they fall on them.
O Father, what is Death? We sport at eve,
A playmate's lips grow pale, the game stands still,
He goes away in silence; as we gaze,
A trembling sigh is loosened from our lips,
Like to the long vibration in the air
After a spire has struck the hour of one.

We sit together at a rich man's feast,
When, as if beckoned by an unseen hand,
The man whose laugh is loudest in his cups,
Rises with a wild face, and goes away
From mirth into a shroud without a word.
With what pale faces, and how still they go!
What visions see they, and what voices hear?
We only know this buried root of life
Holds still, it knows not why, within its heart
A vague tradition of an upper light,
To which it strives, and, dying, spent and foiled,
It feebly feels it should have borne a flower
'Neath some propitious heaven. Fools, we dwell
Within bleak walls of death, and when we hide
Them with this wretched tapestry of life,
We dream that they are not." A hand was laid
Upon my shoulder; Harry's laughing face,
Filled with his mischievous and merry eyes,
Was thrust in mine. He slapped me, "Rouse thee,
man!

The hour is striking, and your dinner waits.
What is the precious subject of your thoughts?"
"My thoughts?—the charitable snow which cools
A hot volcano's lips; the nurse that takes
Alike the crying and the crowing babe,
And stills them with a kiss." We all arose;
The emptying warehouses had filled the street
With a broad stream; from passage, lane, and court
Gushed tributary rills. We struggled out,
And soon were lost and mingled in the tide:
Within an hour the streets again were brimmed
With the returning flow.

Again we sat,
When bright-eyed Harry cried, "How Time doth fly!
March blustered yesterday, to-day the winds
Are ruffling July's roses, ere the morn
October smites the forests into gold.
Yet there is something good in every time:
Winter with breath like incense, glittering beard
Of icicles, enwrapt in sheet of snow,

Is warm at heart, as in the harvest-fields
Bare Autumn, red with sun."

CHARLES.

And kindlier too:
Hear his great fires, see how his bleak old face
Glows ruddy through the steam of fragrant punch.
Can pensive Spring, a snow-drop in his hand,
A solitary lark above his head,
Laugh like the jovial sinner in his cups?
I vote for Winter! Why, you know the "Crown,"
The rows of pewter winking in the light,
The mighty egg-flip at the sanded bar,
The nine-pins, skittles, silent dominoes,
The bellied landlord with his purple head,
Like a red cabbage on December morn
Crusted with snow. His buxom daughter, Bess—
A dahlia, not a rosebud—she who bears
The foaming porter to the guests, and laughs

The loudest at their wit. Can any Summer
Build you a nest like that?

JAMES.

Oft at night,
Weary with beating the black Calder streams,
I dropped into your cozy paradise.
Last week poor Horton died, who sat therein
As constant as a saint within his niche.
I saw him often, heard his glorious talk,
But ere the midnight grew into the morn,
He seemed a mighty angel sent from God
Standing before us—drunk; a sinful song
Staining his radiant lips. I often sat
At those wild drinking bouts, which seemed divine
In a great flash of wit—and rose next morn,
Throat like the parched Sahara, and each ear
Loud as a cotton mill. The o'er-spurred jade
Fell 'neath the rider, and, like all the world,

I found too late the price of loud delights—
Honey in which the bees have left their stings.

MAX.

Ah! he was brightest at the noon of night.
His mind by day was like a common dell,
Through which the clown goes whistling with his cart;
You looked around, but could see nothing more,
Than in a thousand places that you knew:
But with the night, there stole from every leaf,
Where they lay coiled in sleep, dim troops of sylphs,
Fays, and all frolic shapes, and 'neath the moon
Stood Queen Titania and her fairy court.
It is the proudest memory of my youth,
That I was his familiar, and beloved,
And knew his stream of life from fount to sea.
Hope flew before him like a setting sun;
And as he smiled on realms of rosy gold,
From out the heaven there fell a desolate night,

Filled with the welter of the lonely sea,
With wind and spray in his unsheltered hair.
I kept the key of his locked heart for years—
Could ope it when I chose. He loved not Song
With that most pure and undivided love
Which only wins her. Song fled on before;
He followed. Pleasure, naked to the waist,
With high-flushed cheeks and loose dishevelled hair,
Flung herself 'cross his path; she clasped his knees;
He saw her beauty, and he was undone—
His strong heart melted. It was never his,
That terriblest of virtues, Truthfulness;
That pure, high Constancy which flies right on,
As swerveless as a bullet to its mark;
Patience, that with a weary smile can bear
A load that crushes weak complaint to earth—
Patience, that eats the ripened ears, while Haste
Battens upon the green. Yet worth he had,
And strove as far as in him lay, to turn
This smoke of life to clear poetic flame;

To put a something of celestial light
Round the familiar face of every-day.
He plunged from off this crumbling shoal of Time,
Struck for the coast of Fame—with stiffened limbs
Went down in sight of land.

JOHN.

I saw him once,
And, by my faith, he talked us all asleep.
The only things that struck me were his eyes,
That with their brightness held you from his face;
The thought stood in them ere 't was spoken; Wit
Laughed on you from the windows ere she danced
Out on you from the door.

HARRY.

I've heard men speak
Of Horton with such pity in their tones,

That I conceived he had been cruelly hurt
By fortune in his youth.

MAX.

As I have said,
I knew him as myself, and loved him more,
And so my knowledge is more intimate
Than yours, or yours, or any's in the world.
Love will dwell daily with Indifference,
Sleep in one room and at one table sit,
And never speak. Love is but known to Love.
For years his heart was darkened like a grave
By a sepulchral yew. While yet a child,
He had a playmate in his sunny sports;
Inseparable they were as sun and shade.
From childhood's tender sheath there burst at once
A lily-woman—sweetly grave with thoughts
Till now unknown; made silent by a heart
So full and strange, that at a passing tone,

The noiseless falling of an autumn leaf,
It trembled into tears. I often thought,
In the prophetic sorrow of her face,
Her wan pathetic smiles, more sad than tears,
I gazed upon the countenance which awed
The herdsman on the dark Judæan hills
When Jephtha's daughter passed. And so she walked
Vestured in silence; wheresoe'er she went
Loud voices drooped, her beauty carried peace
Into rude discord's heart—and had she bent
Above a soldier from the bloody trench,
The fleeting spirit would have left a smile
Behind it, on the face.
                    One summer day
He lay upon a tower in leafy Kent
Watching a lazy river; glorious leagues
Of woods yet gleaming with a falling shower,
O'er which a rainbow strode; a red-tiled town
Set in a tender film of azure smoke,
And here and there upon the little heights

A windmill turning its preposterous arms
Within the silent noon; the line of sea
That closed the whole. Upon the wall he lay,
Without a wish or trouble in the world.
Her presence filled the universe like light,
And, like an indolent emperor, he lolled
Upon a couch of happiness and love.
So when the sun sank flaming in the west,
He wrote, with a fond smile upon his lips,
(His marriage-day was laughing in his face,)
" The third night hence I start,—that summer night
When you are wakened by an ache of bliss
To some great happiness, and know not what
Until the truth leaps up, think, dearest, think
That I am flying to you through the night
At sixty miles an hour—and that my heart
Outflies the flying train."

The fatal sun
Sucked vapours from the marsh. From morn till eve
The streets were huddled in a yellow fog,

Through which the lamps burned beamlessly and dim.
'Mid household duties sat she hour by hour
With eyes that fed on something far away;
A half smile hovering round her happy lips
Like a bright butterfly around a flower,
Touching, yet settling not. The hour drew near—
Her bliss disturbed her as she sat alone—
She sought relief in friends, and rose at last
With fond and hurried heart. They went with her.
"Don't take the river, Cousin, 'tis so dark."
"It is the shortest way—good night, good night."
They plead, she broke from them, they called to her,
She tossed a laughing answer from the dark.
The girls returned through thick mist-blinded streets,
And sat 'mid music in delighted rooms,
While she groped weeping in night's foggy heart.

Her father, mother, and the new-arrived
Sat in a happy knot. His coming stirred
The constant fire of love within their hearts,

Which crackled and blazed higher. Much he talked
Of London, of its streets, its bridges, crowds;
St. Paul's, the broad moon sailing o'er the dome;
The rich-carved Abbey with its thousand frets
And pinnacles, religious with the dead;
Of the brave spirits who go up to woo
That terrible City whose neglect is death,
Whose smile is fame; the prosperous one who sits
Sole in the summer sun, the crowd who die
Unmentioned, as a wave which forms and breaks
On undiscovered shores. Hour passed on hour,
And gradual each apprehensive lip
Grew silent with concern; then, as they sat,
Like fern-leaves troubled by a sudden wind,
Their hearts were shaken by a speechless fear;
Each read the terror in the other's face.
They searched with lights, they madly called her name—
Night heard, and, conscience-stricken, held its breath,
And listened wild. At last in the bleared morn,

They saw a something white within the stream—
He raised his drowned bride in distracted arms.

A boat with a sweet freight of singing girls,
At rosy eve, when oars are still, will pause,
Then float down with the stream. His merriest talk
Flagged oft, and unpropelled, would ever turn
Into the current of his soul which set,
Constant toward his grief. One afternoon
We wandered forth toward the Raven's Hill,
Whence we might watch the sunset fill the vale.
A silent sea of plenty laved its feet;
We climbed with laughter up its pleasant sides;
But when we reached its lone and heathy head,
We found it haunted by a querulous bird,
Aye wheeling round and round.
Gloom, like a curtain, dropped from brow to chin.
We saw the tawny valley, here and there
Sheaf-dotted fields; a silent string of carts
Creeping along the whitened country road;

Contented cottage smoke; a shot, and lo!
Into the sunset the disturbèd rooks
Arose in noisy clouds from trees that kept
A great man's house a secret. He did not speak;
I felt that something hung upon his heart.
When the great sunset burned itself away,
There lay within the sleepy evening sky
Dark purple slips of cloud, and shallow pools
Of drowsy and most melancholy light.
We sauntered homeward by the clacking mill:
Back from the road we saw the ragged wall,
The broken windows in the haunted house,
And the old rooks' nests in the ruined elms:
Silence grew pain. Sudden, the harvest moon
Stood at our backs, and threw long spears of light
Before us 'mong the shades; at that he drew
The sluice of silence and his life rushed forth—
Its grief, despair, anguish, and clinging hope.
His heart was not, as men conceived, a fair
Of clowns and jugglers, gongs and blaring brass,

But a lone place of tombs and cypresses,
Asleep in silence 'neath the moon of death.
He was a broken and time-crumbled tower,
With sere grass sighing in the evening wind,
Round which a pale ghost flits.

JAMES.

And then his song—
You used to like it, Harry: give it now.

HARRY.

On the Sabbath-day,
Through the churchyard old and grey,
Over the crisp and yellow leaves, I held my rustling way;
And amid the words of mercy, falling on my soul like balms,
'Mid the gorgeous storms of music—in the mellow organ-calms,

'Mid the upward streaming prayers, and the rich and
solemn psalms,
I stood careless, Barbara.

My heart was otherwhere
While the organ shook the air,
And the priest, with outspread hands, blessed the people
with a prayer;
But, when rising to go homeward, with a mild and
saint-like shine
Gleamed a face of airy beauty with its heavenly eyes
on mine—
Gleamed and vanished in a moment—O that face was
surely thine
Out of heaven, Barbara!

O pallid, pallid face!
O earnest eyes of grace!
When last I saw thee, dearest, it was in another
place.

You came running forth to meet me with my love-gift
on your wrist:
The flutter of a long white dress, then all was lost in
mist—
A purple stain of agony was on the mouth I kissed,
That wild morning, Barbara.

I searched, in my despair,
Sunny noon and midnight air;
I could not drive away the thought that you were
lingering there.
O many and many a winter night I sat when you were
gone,
My worn face buried in my hands, beside the fire alone—
Within the dripping churchyard, the rain plashing on
your stone,
You were sleeping, Barbara.

'Mong angels, do you think
Of the precious golden link

I clasped around your happy arm while sitting by yon
brink?
Or when that night of gliding dance, of laughter and
guitars,
Was emptied of its music, and we watched, through
latticed bars,
The silent midnight heaven creeping o'er us with its stars,
Till the day broke, Barbara?

In the years I've changed;
Wild and far my heart hath ranged,
And many sins and errors now have been on me
avenged;
But to you I have been faithful, whatsoever good I
lacked:
I loved you, and above my life still hangs that love
intact—
Your love the trembling rainbow, I the reckless
cataract—
Still I love you, Barbara.

Yet, love, I am unblest;
With many doubts opprest,
I wander like a desert wind, without a place of rest.
Could I but win you for an hour from off that starry shore,
The hunger of my soul were stilled, for Death hath told you more
Than the melancholy world doth know; things deeper than all lore
You could teach me, Barbara.

In vain, in vain, in vain,
You will never come again.
There droops upon the dreary hills a mournful fringe of rain;
The gloaming closes slowly round, loud winds are in the tree,
Round selfish shores for ever moans the hurt and wounded sea,

There is no rest upon the earth, peace is with Death
and thee,
Barbara!

MAX.

I thank you for your silence—for his sake.

CHARLES.

Why, he has told his story in his song!

MAX.

Better than I can. Through that window look
Into the ruined house.

CHARLES.

I picture Art
As some great captive in a gloomy cell,
Who strives in vain to satisfy himself,

By carving every inch of wall and roof
With images of former state, and shapes
That haunt him with their beauty; and, unsought,
There starts beneath his chisel—saddening all,
Freezing the lovely groups of singing girls,
Bursting through every bunch of leaf and flower—
Strange images of grief.

JAMES.

Love, hope, and joy,
Familiar things enough to you and me,
Take a strange glory from the poet's mind:
The white and common daylight, streaming through
A rich cathedral window dim with saints,
Falls on the clasped hands of a stony knight
In palpitating crimson; and the gust
That rudely smites the Æolian harp departs
In melancholy music. Life is the soil,
And song the flower which—

JOHN.

Stop, for Heaven's sake,—
All that has been said a hundred thousand times,
And will be said as often when you're dead.
Now, when we cannot do a noble deed,
Let us be silent. In larger-hearted times
Men stood with Nature face to face, and wrought—
Such love and passion in each fervid stroke—
Their glory, our despair. To us are left
But empty wonder, admiration vain.
Eternal Nature in her pomp goes past;
These giants stand up in the very front
And hide her from us; we but guess the sight
From their adoring murmurs. We live on them,
Feed on their thoughts; each of us strives to speak
The finest words about them. Poor fungi of a day
On trunks of greatness! To our graves we walk
In the thick footprints of departed men.

Life's fire, however high or low it burns—
To cheer a cottage or to fright a realm—
Goes out in worthless ashes at the last.
O! villanous Custom makes the muse's song
Stale as the common highway; steals the gold
From Julia's tresses, which once lit the world;
Makes dear friends smiling in each other's face,
Deem each a tiresome fool; the preacher crying
Of death and judgment,—from which we are divided
But by this thin partition of a breath,—
A pleasant buzzing in a drowsy ear
In a soft-cushion'd pew.

HARRY.

I'll prophesy—
Who'll say me nay?—that in the next Review,
As far off from his subject as he can,
Running a mile that he may leap a yard,
Your critic starts off thus:—" 'Tis not to sing

The dance of stars, the lovely year of flowers,
From the pure snowdrop peeping from the mould
Yet wet with wintry rains, to tiger-lilies
Fierce in their beauty, and tall hollyhocks
On fire through all their length, the poet comes.
They say that song is laid in Byron's grave!
As long as lightning glimmers on the hills,
Song shall be heard; as long as fields are green,
And skies are blue, and woman's face is fair."
Now there is nothing very new in this;
As well remind a man with cheek and nose
Blue with the east wind, that the day is cold.
But lo! he rises to a higher mood:—
"Life is enriched and multiplied by song:
Song re-creates the people of the past,
For one immortal moment we are they,
And one blood beats in all. How dear to man
Is aught of man! Old Time, who frets to dust
The princely circumstance and cloth of gold,
Can never filch the blush from Juliet's cheek,

Or stale the rapture of bold Romeo's kiss—
We touch her lips with him. The workman toils
At his rude craft, goes to his low-roofed home,
Sits at his evening meal; the poet enters
Clothed in the strange sweet light which is his gift—
The poor man starts; he has lived all his days
With beauty, and with grandeur, and with power,
Unrecognised till now." Bald talk like this
(Though, I confess it, not so neatly said)
Besets us everywhere; if well for once—
Repeated, 'tis as if we supped with Jones,
Next eve with Brown, and found the self-same roast
Gracing both tables,—which it sometimes does,
Hired from the butcher in the other street.

CHARLES.

With what a will these fellows cuff, maltreat,
And pound the innocent air!

JAMES.

Is it not strange,
That Horton, filled with purifying sorrow,
Should err so far?

JOHN.

Most wondrous—in a world
Where every sleek and purple-visaged priest
Declaims 'gainst luxury, and dexterous men
Change but their vices and are virtuous!
He—'tis the common fashion of his kind—
Put what he had of goodness in his verse,
And left none for his life. He knew his game:—
Stuff your shop-window thickly with your goods;
The world ne'er marks the empty shelves behind.
Grief proudlier dwells in sounding lines, than in
A faithful heart. What beauty would not choose

To sit and smile within a balcony
Full in the seeing of the public eye,
Rather than in a hut?

MAX.

You do him wrong:
His errors rose from no ill-biassed soul,
Nor appetite depraved. The finer nerve,
The mournful wisdom gather'd by an eye
That saw the wither'd autumn in the fruit
Glowing upon the bough, were more to blame.
Death look'd upon him through the eyes of Love;
No mercy veil'd for him those dreadful orbs;
And often, to escape their silent gaze,
He hid in Riot's arms. We often see
Powers left unused, or in their uses lost.
The ponderous axe leans 'gainst the idle wall
Till rust consumes it; and the invisible edge,
That could divide the weightless gossamer

Nor shake a trembling dewdrop from its threads,
Must hew the rock. Whenc'er Apollo draws
The arrow thirsting for the Python's blood
Home to the quivering head, his flashing limbs
Are palsied by a touch. The heavens seem
To mar as wilfully their creature man,
As one who limns a face, on which the world
Could stand at gaze cheated of pain and time;
Then lets, before the smiling hues are dry,
His careless sleeve slur all as off he goes.
Nature, who makes the perfect rose and bird,
Has never made the full and perfect man.
In every worthiness there is a flaw,
That, like a crack across a mirror's face,
Impairs its value: cunningly, she lets
Nothing have knowledge of its own defect:
To keep us living she must cozen us:
The dun toad panting in the cool of eve,
The eagle bathing in the bursting dawn,
Are each content alike. Without these toys—

Ambition, pleasure, wealth, opinion, love,
Which fill our eyes, and hide us from ourselves—
Like lonely children we should die with fright
At utter nothingness. His muse had breath,
And loved so well this old familiar earth,
She ne'er desired to walk in other stars,
Nor dwell 'neath ampler seasons; and his verse,
Like a rich marriage with its minstrelsy,
Or Neptune with a sound of weltering waves,
Had still a lordly march. Had he but lived—
Yet, very vain and fruitless is the wish!
Death holds up in his hand the lamp by which
We note the prostrate strength, and guess what all
At strain could reach. He stood so high, there seemed
Between his footing and the immortal mount
A single step: however slight the space,
It was to him a gulf impassable,
And wide as death. Yet 'tis a loving thought,—
Had Fate not so untimely reap'd the field,

Its hasty crop of poppies had been drown'd
In heavy ears of wheat.

ARTHUR.

A friend of mine,
At whose rich table Horton often sat,
When fond men dream'd they saw around his head
The apparition of the future light,
Told me, he was in spirit hot and quick;
Weak as a flower that sways with ev'ry wind:
That, like the sensitive leaf, his vanity
Shrank from the slightest touch; and that he turn'd
From those who loved him, and reproved him, too,
And found his heaven in a tavern's laugh.

MAX.

With their own cotton may your friends be choked!
O, 'tis the crowning baseness of the fiend

To taunt the fallen Eve! They gave him wine;
They pampered, flattered him; they struck the light
In that combustible and tinder house,
And, when 'twas sheeted in devouring flame,
They, in the fashion of our dearest friends,
Cried, "Fire!" to all the world. You have a friend:
Touch your friend's heart with a poor orphan's cry,
He sips his wine unmoved; touch now his purse—
Look, how he winces! He is vital there.
O, rare to hear this Cotton-bag, with soul
Scarce saucer-deep, rate Horton for his faults!
Had he his heart one hour, within his life
'Twere like the famous tear that Xerxes shed—
The one thing worth remembering. So they judge
This larger spirit, fresh from Nature's heart
As a volcano; compound perilous
Of hell and heaven, wrath and woman's tears!
He sank beneath them in his passionate sins;
His goodness sang a skylark o'er their heads,
And Heaven stood to hear.

His silent grave
Rebukes these words. But let us ne'er forget
His errors darkened in the very blaze
And sunlight of his virtues. A slur of mire
Sits more conspicuous on the captain's steel,
Than on the battle-worn and dinted mail
Of the rude man-at-arms. His sin of sins
Was ne'er to be the master of himself.
His heart, which should have constant been to song—
True, as the monsoon breathing day and night
To China and the Isles—was drawn aside
By pomps and pleasures dancing upon graves
To Vanity's soft pipe. When erring man
Strays from his duty, Heaven ever strives
To bring him back. 'T is writ, when Moses fled,
And drowned remembrance of the groaning tribes
In the sweet bleating of the Midian flocks—
The hand which should break Egypt, sound asleep
'Mid Zipporah's long tresses—God appear'd
Within the burning bush. Alas! for him

Who cannot hear the voice; he turns from Hope,
And gives his hand to Ruin. The Muse disdains
A lukewarm lover. He who could not sit
And sing contented in a desert isle,
His audience, the mute trees and wandering winds,
His joy, the grace and beauty of his song,
Should never lift his voice 'mong mortal men.
The noble artist finds enough reward,
While the pure nymph is growing from the stone,
In the sweet smile with which she blesses him
For loveliness and immortality.
He coveted the Muse's smile—but more,
Earth's praise; for Fame's consummate fruit, which ne'er
Has cool'd the fever of a living lip,
Which ripens slowly through laborious years,
Then, heavy with its sweetness and its bloom,
Falls on a grave, he could not wait; so pluck'd
Crude Reputation's green and bastard crab,
Which set his teeth on edge. This error soured

His native goodness. Slow he fell from light,
And year by year the heavens seemed farther off,
And human faces less divine. He died
With a wild jest; 'twas the last flash of flame
Upon the blackened brand. Was this ship stored,
And sent forth glorious only to enrich
The wasteful waves? O, surely to advance
The far result which Heaven shapes from out
The multitudinous clash and roar of things,
This man might have been used—not thrown aside,
As in a loud and clanging tournament,
A splintered lance. But Heaven darkly works;
A pale man bears about a martyr's heart,
And never finds his fire; while one burns high
With a recanting soul. The patriot's head
Wastes on a pole above a gate of slaves
In sun and rain, while he who only sought
The awful glitter of the diadem,
Stands crowned, with acclamations of the free
Rising like incense round him. On the sands

Jove lolls, and listens to the sleepy surge,
His right arm boltless, and that brow, whose frown
Could shake Olympus, naked as the peak
That fronts the sunset; while a baby-hand
Clutches the thunder. Yet through all we know
This tangled skein is in the hands of One
Who sees the end from the beginning—He
Shall yet unravel all.

Our stream of talk
Here split in petty rills which ran to waste,
And sank in silence. When that swallows' haunt,
St. Stephen's, with its showers of silvery chimes,
Stood black against the red dilated sun,
Labour laid down his tools and went away.
The park was loud with games: clear laughter, shrieks,
Came from the rings of girls amid the trees;
The cricketers were eager at their play;
The stream was dotted with the swimmers' heads;
Gay boats flashed up and down. The level sun

Poured o'er the sward a farewell gush of light,
And Sport transfigured stood! I hurried on,
Through all the mirth, to where the river ran,
In the grey evening, 'tween the hanging woods,
With a soul-soothing murmur. Seated there,
The darkness closing round me, I could see
A lonely angler like a heron stand,
And hear the blackbird piping to the eve,
And smell the wild-rose on the dewy air.
I reached the park hours later,—what a change!
The full-moon filled the universal night;
The stream ran white with lustre; walks and trees
Threw their long shadows; a few kine lay dark
In lanes and squares of moonlight; far away
The pallid rim of night was touched with fires;
Stillness was deep as death. "The noisy day
Wheels into silence; and this wave of life,
Crowned with its fretting foam, subsides at last
On shores without a sound. And this our Time—
With thrones tyrannic girt by seas of steel;

Wild nations starting up from sleep to chase
A dream of liberty through blood and fire ;
White faces down in dungeons cursing kings ;
Battle, and wintry siege, and frozen hosts—
Will sink and lose itself in utter peace
Like water spilt on sand. And History,
A mournful follower in the track of man,
Whose path is over ruin and the grave,
May linger for a moment in this place
Beside a worn inscription and be sad."

Across the moonlight spaces and the shades
I walked in silence, through pale silver streets,
Athwart a desolate and moon-bleached square,
Over a white and solitary bridge,
Until I reached my home. I oped the door,
And ere it closed, I heard a distant spire
Start in its sleep, and murmur of an hour.

GLASGOW.

GLASGOW.

Sing, Poet, 'tis a merry world;
That cottage smoke is rolled and curled
    In sport, that every moss
Is happy, every inch of soil;—
Before *me* runs a road of toil
    With my grave cut across.
Sing, trailing showers and breezy downs—
I know the tragic hearts of towns.

City! I am true son of thine;
Ne'er dwelt I where great mornings shine
    Around the bleating pens;
Ne'er by the rivulets I strayed,

And ne'er upon my childhood weighed
The silence of the glens.
Instead of shores where ocean beats,
I hear the ebb and flow of streets.

Black Labour draws his weary waves,
Into their secret-moaning caves;
But with the morning light,
That sea again will overflow
With a long weary sound of woe,
Again to faint in night.
Wave am I in that sea of woes,
Which, night and morning, ebbs and flows.

I dwelt within a gloomy court,
Wherein did never sunbeam sport;
Yet there my heart was stirr'd—
My very blood did dance and thrill,
When on my narrow window-sill,
Spring lighted like a bird.

Poor flowers—I watched them pine for weeks,
With leaves as pale as human cheeks.

Afar, one summer, I was borne;
Through golden vapours of the morn,
I heard the hills of sheep:
I trod with a wild ecstasy
The bright fringe of the living sea:
And on a ruined keep
I sat, and watched an endless plain
Blacken beneath the gloom of rain.

O fair the lightly sprinkled waste,
O'er which a laughing shower has raced!
O fair the April shoots!
O fair the woods on summer days,
While a blue hyacinthine haze
Is dreaming round the roots!
In thee, O City! I discern
Another beauty, sad and stern.

Draw thy fierce streams of blinding ore,
Smite on a thousand anvils, roar
 Down to the harbour-bars;
Smoulder in smoky sunsets, flare
On rainy nights, with street and square
 Lie empty to the stars.
From terrace proud to alley base
I know thee as my mother's face.

When sunset bathes thee in his gold,
In wreaths of bronze thy sides are rolled,
 Thy smoke is dusky fire;
And, from the glory round thee poured,
A sunbeam like an angel's sword
 Shivers upon a spire.
Thus have I watched thee, Terror! Dream!
While the blue Night crept up the stream.

The wild Train plunges in the hills,
He shrieks across the midnight rills;

Streams through the shifting glare,
The roar and flap of foundry fires,
That shake with light the sleeping shires;
And on the moorlands bare,
He sees afar a crown of light
Hang o'er thee in the hollow night.

At midnight, when thy suburbs lie
As silent as a noonday sky,
When larks with heat are mute,
I love to linger on thy bridge,
All lonely as a mountain ridge,
Disturbed but by my foot;
While the black lazy stream beneath,
Steals from its far-off wilds of heath.

And through thy heart, as through a dream,
Flows on that black disdainful stream;
All scornfully it flows,
Between the huddled gloom of masts,

Silent as pines unvexed by blasts—
'Tween lamps in streaming rows.
O wondrous sight! O stream of dread!
O long dark river of the dead!

Afar, the banner of the year
Unfurls: but dimly prisoned here,
'Tis only when I greet
A dropt rose lying in my way,
A butterfly that flutters gay
Athwart the noisy street,
I know the happy Summer smiles
Around thy suburbs, miles on miles.

'T were neither pæan now, nor dirge,
The flash and thunder of the surge
On flat sands wide and bare;
No haunting joy or anguish dwells
In the green light of sunny dells,
Or in the starry air.

Alike to me the desert flower,
The rainbow laughing o'er the shower.

While o'er thy walls the darkness sails,
I lean against the churchyard rails;
Up in the midnight towers
The belfried spire, the street is dead,
I hear in silence over head
The clang of iron hours:
It moves me not—I know her tomb
Is yonder in the shapeless gloom.

All raptures of this mortal breath,
Solemnities of life and death,
Dwell in thy noise alone:
Of me thou hast become a part—
Some kindred with my human heart
Lives in thy streets of stone;
For we have been familiar more
Than galley-slave and weary oar.

The beech is dipped in wine; the shower
Is burnished; on the swinging flower
        The latest bee doth sit.
The low sun stares through dust of gold,
And o'er the darkening heath and wold
        The large ghost-moth doth flit.
In every orchard Autumn stands,
With apples in his golden hands.

But all these sights and sounds are strange;
Then wherefore from thee should I range?
        Thou hast my kith and kin:
My childhood, youth, and manhood brave;
Thou hast that unforgotten grave
        Within thy central din.
A sacredness of love and death
Dwells in thy noise and smoky breath.

SQUIRE MAURICE.

SQUIRE MAURICE.

I THREW from off me yesterday
The dull life I am doomed to wear—
A worn-out garment dim and bare,
And left it in my chambers grey:
The salt breeze wanders in my hair
Beside the splendour of the main:
Ere on the deep three sunsets burn,
To the old chambers I return,
And put it on again.
An old coat, worn for many a year,
No wonder it is something dear!

Ah, year by year life's fire burns out,
And year by year life's stream runs dry:

The wild deer dies within the blood,
The falcon in the eye.
And Hope, who sang miraculous songs
Of what should be, like one inspired,
How she should right the ancient wrongs,
(The generous fool !) grows hoarse and tired;
And turns from visions of a world renewed,
To dream of tripled rents, fair miles of stream and wood.
The savage horse, that leads
His tameless herd across the endless plain,
Is taught at last, with sullen heart, to strain
Beneath his load, nor quiver when he bleeds.
We cheat ourselves with our own lying eyes,
We chase a fleeting mirage o'er the sand,
Across a grave the smiling phantom flies,
O'er which we fall with a vain-clutching hand.
What matter—if we heave laborious breath,
And crack our hearts and sinews, groan and weep,
The pain of life but sweetens death,
The hardest labour brings the soundest sleep.

On bank and brae how thick they grow,
The self-same clumps, the self-same dyes,
The primroses of long ago—
But ah! the altered eyes!
I dream they are the very flowers,
Warm with the sun, wet with the showers,
Which, years ago, I used to pull
Returning from the murmuring school.
Sweet Nature is a mother ever more;
A thousand tribes are breathing on the shore;
The pansy blows beside the rock,
The globe-flower, where the eddy swirls;
And on this withered human stock
Burst rosy boys and girls.
Sets Nature little store
On that which once she bore?
Does she forget the old, in rapture bear the new?
Are ye the flowers that grew
In other seasons? Do they e'er return,
The men who build the cities on the plain?—

Or must my tearless eyeballs burn
For ever o'er that early urn,
Ne'er to be cooled by a delicious dew?
Let me take back my pain
Unto my heart again;
Before I can recover that I lack
The world must be rolled back.

Inland I wander slow,
Mute with the power the earth and heaven wield:
A black spot sails across the golden field,
And through the air a crow.
Before me wavers spring's first butterfly;
From out the sunny noon there starts the cuckoo's cry;
The daisied meads are musical with lambs;
Some play, some feed, some, white as snow-flakes, lie
In the deep sunshine, by their silent dams.
The road grows wide and level to the feet;
The wandering woodbine through the hedge is drawn,
Unblown its streaky bugles dim and sweet;

Knee-deep in fern stand startled doe and fawn,
And lo ! there gleams upon a spacious lawn
An Earl's marine retreat.
A little foot-path quivers up the height,
And what a vision for a townsman's sight !
A village, peeping from its orchard bloom,
With lowly roofs of thatch, blue threads of smoke,
O'erlooking all, a parsonage of white.
I hear the smithy's hammer, stroke on stroke ;
A steed is at the door ; the rustics talk,
Proud of the notice of the gaitered groom ;
A shallow river breaks o'er shallow falls.
Beside the ancient sluice that turns the mill
The lusty miller bawls ;
The parson listens in his garden-walk,
The red-cloaked woman pauses on the hill.
This is a place, you say, exempt from ill,
A paradise, where, all the loitering day,
Enamoured pigeons coo upon the roof,
Where children ever play.—

Alas ! Time's webs are rotten, warp and woof ;
Rotten his cloth of gold, his coarsest wear :
Here, black-eyed Richard ruins red-cheeked Moll,
Indifferent as a lord to her despair.
The broken barrow hates the prosperous dray ;
And, for a padded pew in which to pray,
The grocer sells his soul.

This cosy hostelrie a visit craves;
Here will I sit awhile,
And watch the heavenly sunshine smile
Upon the village graves.
Strange is this little room in which I wait,
With its old table, rough with rustic names.
'Tis summer now ; instead of blinking flames,
Sweet-smelling ferns are hanging o'er the grate.
With curious eyes I pore
Upon the mantel-piece, its precious wares,
Glazed Scripture prints in black lugubrious frames,
Filled with old Bible lore :

The whale is casting Jonah on the shore;
Pharaoh is drowning in the curly wave;
And to Elijah sitting at his cave,
The hospitable ravens fly in pairs,
Celestial food within their horny beaks;
On a slim David, with great pinky cheeks,
A towered Goliath stares.
Here will I sit at peace:
While, piercing through the window's ivy-veil,
A slip of sunshine smites the amber ale;
And as the wreaths of fragrant smoke increase,
I'll read the letter which came down to-day.
Ah, happy Maurice! while in chambers dun,
I pore o'er deeds and parchments growing grey,
Each glowing realm that spreads beneath the sun
Is but a paradise where you may play.
I am a bonded workman, you are free;
In your blood's hey-day—mine is early cold.
Life is rude furze at best; the sea-breeze wrings
And eats my branches on the bitter lea;

But you have root in dingle fat and old,
Fat with decayings of a hundred springs,
And blaze all splendid in your points of gold,
And in your heart a linnet sits and sings.

"Unstable as the wind, infirm as foam,
I envy, Charles, your calmness and your peace;
The eye that marks its quarry from afar,
The heart that stoops on it and smites it down.
I, struggling in a dim and obscure net,
Am but enmeshed the more. When you were here,
My spirit often burned to tell you all;
I urged the horse up to the leap, it shied
At something in the hedge. This must not last;
In shame and sorrow, ere I sleep to-night,
I'll shrive my inmost soul.
I have knelt, and sworn
By the sweet heavens—I have madly prayed
To be by them forsaken, when I forsake
A girl whose lot should be to sleep content

Upon a peasant's breast, and toil all day
'Mong flaxen-headed children. She sits to-night,
When all the little town is lost in dream,
Her lax hands sunk in her neglected work,
Thinking of me. Smile not, my man of law,
Who, with a peering candle, walkest through
Black places in men's hearts, which only hear
The foot of conscience at the dead of night!
Her name might slip into my holiest prayer;
Her breath has come and gone upon my cheek,
Yet I dare stand before my mother's face,
Dare look into the heavenly eyes that yearn
For ever through a mist of golden hair,
With no shame on my brow. 'Tis not that way
My trouble looks. Yet, friend, in simple truth,
Could this thing be obliterated quite,
Expunged for ever, like a useless cloak
I'd fling off my possessions, and go forth,
My roof the weeping heaven.

Though I would die

Rather than give her pain, I grimly smile
To think, were I assured this horrid dream
Which poisons day to me, would only prove
A breath upon the mirror of her mind—
A moment dim, then gone (an issue which,
Could *I* have blotted out all memory,
Would let me freely breathe)—this love would turn
To bitterest gall of hate. O Vanity,
Thou god, who on the altar thou hast built
Pilest myrrh and frankincense, appliest the flame,
Then snuff'st the smoky incense, high and calm!
Thou nimble Proteus of all human shapes!
Malvolio, cross-gartered in the sun,
The dying martyr, gazing from his fire
Upon the opened heavens, filled with crowds
Of glorious angel-faces:—thou art all
We smile at, all we hymn! For thee we blush,
For thee shed noble tears! The glowing coal,
O'er which the frozen beggar spreads his hands,
Is of one essence with the diamond,

That on the haughty forehead of a queen
Trembles with dewy light. Could *I*, through pain,
Give back the peace I stole, my heart would leap;
Could *she* forget me and regain content—
How deeply I am wronged!

" Is it the ancient trouble of my house
That makes the hours so terrible? Other men
Live to more purpose than those monstrous weeds
That drink a breadth of sunshine, and give back
Nor hue nor fragrance; but my spirit droops,
A dead and idle banner from its staff,
Unstirred by any wind. Within a cell,
Without a straw to play with, or a nail
To carve my sorrow on the gloomy stone,
I sit and watch, from stagnant day to day,
The bloated spider hanging on its thread,
The dull fly on the wall. The blessed sleep
For which none are too poor; the sleep that comes
So sweetly to the weary labouring man,

The march-worn soldier on the naked ground,
The martyr in the pauses of the rack,
Drives me through forests full of dreadful eyes,
Flings me o'er precipices, makes me kneel,
A sentenced man, before the dark platoon,
Or lays me helpless in the dim embrace
Of formless horror. Long ago, two foes
Lay in the yellow evening in their gore:
Like a malignant fury, that wild hour
Threw madness in the river of our blood:
Though it has run for thrice a century,
Been sweetened all the way by mothers' tears,
'Tis poisoned until now.

See how I stand
Delaying on the brink, like one who fears
And yet would meet the chill! When you were here
You saw a smoking-cap among my books;
A fond and fluttering letter badly spelt,
Each sentence headed with a little *i*,
Came with it, read with a blush, tossed in the fire,

Nor answered yet. Can you not now detect
The snail's slime on the rose?
This miserable thing
Grew round me like the ivy round the oak;
Sweet were its early creeping rings, though now
I choke, from knotted root to highest bough.
In those too happy days I could not name
This strange new thing which came upon my youth,
But yielded to its sweetness. Fling it off?
Trample it down? Bid me pluck out the eye
In which the sweet world dwells!—One night she wept;
It seemed so strange that *I* could make her weep:
Kisses may lie, but tears are surely true.
Then unbelief came back in solitude,
And Love grew cruel; and to be assured
Cried out for tears, and with a shaking hand
And a wild heart that could have almost burst
With utter tenderness, yet would not spare,
He clutched her heart, and at the starting tears
Grew soft with all remorse. For those mad hours

Remembrance frets my heart in solitude,
As the lone mouse when all the house is still
Gnaws at the wainscot.
'Tis a haunting face,
Yet oftentimes I think I love her not;
Love's white hand flutters o'er my spirit's keys
Unkissed by grateful music. Oft I think
The Lady Florence at the county ball,
Quenching the beauties as the lightning dims
The candles in a room, scarce smiles so sweet.
The one oppresses like a crown of gold,
The other gladdens like a beam in spring,
Stealing across a dim field, making blithe
Its daisies one by one.—I deemed that I
Had broke my house of bondage, when one night
The memory of her face came back so sweet,
And stood between me and the printed page;
And phantoms of a thousand happy looks
Smiled from the dark. It was the old weak tale
Which time has told from Adam till this hour:

The slave comes back, takes up his broken chain.
I rode through storm toward the little town;
The minster, gleamed on by the flying moon,
Tolled midnight as I passed. I only sought
To see the line of light beneath her door,
The knowledge of her nearness was so sweet.
Hid in the darkness of the church, I watched
Her window like a shrine: a light came in,
And a soft shadow broke along the roof;
She raised the window and leaned forth awhile.
I could have fallen down and kissed her feet;
The poor dear heart, I knew it could not rest;
I stood between her and the light—my shade
Fell 'cross her silver sphere. The window closed.
When morn with cold bleak crimson laced the east,
Against a stream of raw and rainy wind
I rode back to the Hall.

The play-book tells
How Fortune's slippery wheel in Syracuse
Flung prosperous lordship to the chilly shades,

Heaved serfdom to the sun: in precious silks
Charwomen flounced, and scullions sat and laughed
In golden chairs, to see their fellows play
At football with a crown. Within my heart
In this old house, when all the fiends are here,
The story is renewed. Peace only comes
With a wild ride across the barren downs,
One look upon her face. She ne'er complains
Of my long absences, my hasty speech,—
'Crumbs from thy table are enough for me.'
She only asks to be allowed to lean
Her head against my breast a little while,
And she is paid for all. I choke with tears,
And think myself a devil from the pit
Loved by an angel. O that she would change
This tenderness and drooping-lily look,
The flutter when I come, the unblaming voice,
Wet eyes held up to kiss—one flash of fire,
A moment's start of keen and crimson scorn,
Would make me hers for ever!

I draw my birth
From a long line of gallant gentlemen,
Who only feared a lie—but what is this?
I dare not slight the daughter of a peer;
Her kindred could avenge. Yet I dare play
And palter with the pure soul of a girl
Without friend, who, smitten, speaks no word,
But with a helpless face sinks in the grave
And takes her wrongs to God. Thou dark Sir Ralph,
Who lay with broken brand on Marston Moor,
What think you of this son?

"This prison that I dwell in hath two doors,
Desertion, marriage; both are shut by shame,
And barred by cowardice. A stronger man
Would screw his heart up to the bitter wrench,
And break through either and regain the air.
I cannot give myself or others pain.
I wear a conscience nice and scrupulous,
Which, while it hesitates to draw a tear,

Lets a heart break. Conscience should be clear-eyed,
And look through years: conscience is tenderest oft
When clad in sternness, when it smites to-day,
To stay the ruin which it hears afar
Upon the wind. Pure womanhood is meek—
But which is nobler, the hysterical girl
Weeping o'er flies huddling in slips of sun
On autumn sills, who has not heart enough
To crush a wounded grasshopper and end
Torture at once; or she, with flashing eyes,
Among the cannon, a heroic foot
Upon a fallen breast? My nerveless will
Is like a traitorous second, and deserts
My purpose in the very gap of need.
I groan beneath this cowardice of heart,
Which rolls the evil to be borne to-day
Upon to-morrow, loading it with gloom.
The man who clothes the stony moor with green,
In virtue of the beauty he creates,
Has there a right to dwell. And he who stands

Firm in this shifting sand and drift of things,
And rears from out the wasteful elements
An ordered home, in which the awful Gods,
The lighter Graces, serene Muses, dwell,
Holds in that masterdom the chartered right
To his demesne of Time. But I hold none;
I live by sufferance, am weak and vain
As a shed leaf upon a turbid stream,
Or an abandoned boat which can but drift
Whither the currents draw—to maelstrom, or
To green delicious shores. I should have had
My pendent cradle rocked by laughing winds
Within some innocent and idle isle
Where the sweet bread-fruit ripens and falls down,
Where the swollen pumpkin lolls upon the ground,
The lithe and slippery savage, drenched with oil,
Sleeps in the sun, and life is lazy ease.
But lamentation and complaint are vain:
The skies are stern and serious as doom;
The avalanche is loosened by a laugh;

And he who throws the dice of destiny,
Though with a sportive and unthinking hand,
Must bide the issue, be it life or death.
One path is clear before me. It may lead
O'er perilous rock, 'cross sands without a well,
Through deep and difficult chasms, but therein
The whiteness of the soul is kept, and that,
Not joy nor happiness, is victory.

"Ah, she is not the creature who I dreamed
Should one day walk beside me dearly loved:
No fair majestic woman, void of fear,
And unabashed from purity of heart;
No girl with liquid eyes and shadowy hair,
To sing at twilight like a nightingale,
Or fill the silence with her glimmering smiles,
Deeper than speech or song. She has no birth,
No dowry, graces; no accomplishments,
Save a pure cheek, a fearless innocent brow,
And a true-beating heart. She is no bank

Of rare exotics which o'ercome the sense
With perfumes—only fresh uncultured soil
With a wild-violet grace and sweetness born
Of Nature's teeming foison. Is this not
Enough to sweeten life? Could one not live
On brown bread, clearest water? Is this love
(What idle poets feign in fabling songs)
An unseen god, whose voice is heard but once
In youth's green valleys, ever dead and mute
'Mong manhood's iron hills? A power that comes
On the instant, whelming, like the light that smote
Saul from his horse; never a thing that draws
Its exquisite being from the light of smiles
And low sweet tones and fond companionship?
Brothers and sisters grow up by our sides,
Unfelt and silently are knit to us,
And one flesh with our hearts; would love not grow
In the communion of long-wedded years,
Sweet as the dawning light, the greening spring?
Would not an infant be the marriage priest,

To stand between us and unite our hands,
And bid us love and be obeyed? its life,
A fountain, with a cooling fringe of green
Amid the arid sands, by which we twain
Could dwell in deep content? My sunshine drew
This odorous blossom from the bough; why then
With frosty fingers wither it, and seal up
Sun-ripened fruit within its barren rind,
Killing all sweet delights? I drew it forth:
If there is suffering, let me bear it all.

"A very little goodness goes for much.
Walk 'mong my peasants—every urchin's face
Lights at my coming; girls at cottage-doors
Rise from their work and curtsey as I pass,
And old men bless me with their silent tears!
What have I done for this? I'm kind, they say,
Give coals in winter, cordials for the sick,
And once a fortnight stroke a curly head
Which hides half-frightened in a russet gown.

'Tis easy for the sun to shine. My alms
Are to my riches like a beam to him.
They love me, these poor hinds, though I have ne'er
Resigned a pleasure, let a whim be crossed,
Pinched for an hour the stomach of desire
For one of them. Good Heaven! what am I
To be thus servitored? Am I to range
Like the discourseless creatures of the wood,
Without the common dignity of pain,
Without a pale or limit? To take up love
For its strange sweetness, and whene'er it tires,
Fling it aside as careless as I brush
A gnat from off my arm, and go my way
Untwinged with keen remorse? All this must end.
Firm land at last begins to peer above
The ebbing waves of hesitance and doubt.
Throughout this deepening spring my purpose grows
To flee with her to those young morning lands—
Australia, where the earth is gold, or where
The prairies roll toward the setting sun.

Not Lady Florence with her coronet,
Flinging white arms around me, murmuring
'Husband' upon my breast—not even that
Could make me happy, if I left a grave
On which the shadow of the village spire
Should rest at eve. The pain, if pain there be,
I'll keep locked up within my secret heart,
And wear what joy I have upon my face;
And she shall live and laugh, and never know.

" Come, Brother, at your earliest, down to me.
To-morrow night I sleep at Ferny-Chase:
There, shadowed by the memory of the dead,
We'll talk of this. My thought, mayhap, will take
A different hue, seen in your purer light,
Free from all stain of passion. Ere you come,
Break that false mirror of your ridicule,
Looking in which, the holiest saint beholds
A grinning Jackanapes, and hates himself.
More men hath Laughter driven from the right

Than Terror clad with fire. You have been young,
And know the mystery, that when we love,
We love the thing, not only for itself
But somewhat also for the love we give.
Think of the genial season of your youth
When you dwelt here, and come with serious heart."

So, in that bitter quarter sits the wind:
The village fool could tell, unless it shifts
'Twill bring the rain in fiercest flaws and drifts!
How wise we are, yet blind,
Judging the wood's grain from the outer rind;
Wrapt in the twilight of this prison dim,
He envies me, I envy him!

The stream of my existence boils and leaps
Through broken rainbows 'mong the purple fells,
And breaks its heart 'mid rocks, close-jammed, confined,
And plunges in a chasm black and blind,
To rage in hollow gulfs and iron hells,

And thence escaping, tamed and broken, creeps
Away in a wild sweat of beads and bells.
Though *his* slides lazy through the milky meads,
And once a week the sleepy slow-trailed barge
Rocks the broad water-lilies on its marge,
A dead face wavers from the oozy weeds.
It is but little matter where we dwell,
In fortune's centre, on her utter verge;
Whither to death our weary steps we urge,
Or ride with ringing bridle, golden selle.
Life is one pattern wrought in different hues,
And there is nought to choose
Between its sad and gay—'tis but to groan
Upon a rainy common or a throne,
Bleed 'neath the purple or the peasants' serge.

At his call I will go,
Though it is very little love can do;
In spite of all affection tried and true,
Each man alone must struggle with his woe.

He pities her, for he has done her wrong,
And would repair the evil—noble deed,
To flash and tingle in a minstrel's song,
To move the laughter of our modern breed!
And yet the world is wise; each curve and round
Of custom's road is no result of chance;
It curves but to avoid some treacherous ground,
Some quagmire in the wilds of circumstance;
Nor safely left. The long-drawn caravan
Wavers through heat, then files o'er Mecca's stones;
Far in the blinding desert lie the bones
Of the proud-hearted solitary man.
He marries her, but ere the year has died,—
'Tis an old tale,—they wander to the grave
With hot revolting hearts, yet lashed and tied
Like galley-slave to slave.
Love should not stoop to Love, like prince to lord:
While o'er their heads proud Cupid claps his wings,
Love should meet Love upon the marriage sward,
And kiss, like crowned kings.

If both are hurt, then let them bear the pain
Upon their separate paths; 't will die at last:
The deed of one rash moment may remain
To darken all the future with the past.
And yet I cannot tell,—the beam that kills
The gipsy's fire, kindles the desert flower;
Where he plucks blessings I may gather ills,
And in his sweetest sweet find sourest sour.
If what of wisdom and experience
My years have brought, be either guide or aid,
They shall be his, though to my mournful sense
The lights will steal away from wood and glade;
The garden will be sad with all its glows,
And I shall hear the glistening laurels talk
Of her, as I pass under in the walk,
And my light step will thrill each conscious rose.

The lark hangs high o'er Ferny-Chase
In slant of sun, in twinkle of rain;
Though loud and clear, the song I hear

Is half of joy, and half of pain.
I know by heart the dear old place,
The place where Spring and Summer meet—
By heart, like those old ballad rhymes,
O'er which I brood a million times,
And sink from sweet to deeper sweet.
I know the changes of the idle skies,
The idle shapes in which the clouds are blown;
The dear old place is now before my eyes,
Yea, to the daisy's shadow on the stone.
When through the golden furnace of the heat
The far-off landscape seems to shake and beat,
Within the lake I see old Hodge's cows
Stand in their shadows in a tranquil drowse,
While o'er them hangs a restless steam of flies.
I see the clustered chimneys of the Hall
Stretch o'er the lawn toward the blazing lake;
And in the dewy even-fall
I hear the mellow thrushes call
From tree to tree, from brake to brake.

Ah! when I thither go
I know that my joy-emptied eyes shall see
A white Ghost wandering where the lilies blow,
A Sorrow sitting by the trysting tree.
I kiss this soft curl of her living hair,
'Tis full of light as when she did unbind
Her sudden ringlets, making bright the wind:
'Tis here, but she is—where?
Why do I, like a child impatient, weep?
Delight dies like a wreath of frosted breath;
Though here I toil upon the barren deep,
I see the sunshine yonder lie asleep,
Upon the calm and beauteous shores of Death.
Ah, Maurice, let thy human heart decide,
The first best pilot through distracting jars.
The lowliest roof of love at least will hide
The desolation of the lonely stars.
Stretched on the painful rack of forty years,
I've learned at last the sad philosophy
Of the unhoping heart, unshrinking eye—

God knows; my icy wisdom and my sneers
Are frozen tears!

The day wears, and I go.
Farewell, Elijah! may you heartily dine!
I cannot, David, see your fingers twine
In the long hair of your foe.
Housewife, adieu, Heaven keep your ample form,
May custom never fail;
And may your heart, as sound as your own ale,
Be soured by never a storm!

Though I have travelled now for twice an hour,
I have not heard a bird or seen a flower.
This wild road has a little mountain rill
To sing to it, ah! happier than I.
How desolate the region, and how still
The idle earth looks on the idle sky!
I trace the river by its wandering green;
The vale contracts to a steep pass of fear,

And through the midnight of the pines I hear
The torrent raging down the long ravine.
At last I've reached the summit high and bare;
I fling myself on heather dry and brown:
As silent as a picture lies the town,
Its peaceful smokes are curling in the air;
The bay is one delicious sheet of rose,
And round the far point of the tinted cliffs
I see the long strings of the fishing skiffs
Come home to roost like lines of evening crows.
I can be idle only one day more
As the nets drying on the sunny shore;
Thereafter, chambers, still 'mid thronged resorts,
Strewn books and littered parchments, nought to see,
Save a charwoman's face, a dingy tree,
A fountain plashing in the empty courts.

But let me hasten down this shepherd's track,
The Night is at my back.

THE NIGHT BEFORE THE WEDDING,

OR

TEN YEARS AFTER.

THE NIGHT BEFORE THE WEDDING;

OR,

TEN YEARS AFTER.

THE country ways are full of mire,
The boughs toss in the fading light,
The winds blow out the sunset's fire,
And sudden droppeth down the night.
I sit in this familiar room,
Where mud-splashed hunting squires resort;
My sole companion in the gloom
This slowly dying pint of port.

'Mong all the joys my soul hath known,
'Mong errors over which it grieves,
I sit at this dark hour alone,
Like Autumn mid his wither'd leaves.

This is a night of wild farewells
To all the past; the good, the fair;
To-morrow, and my wedding bells
Will make a music in the air.

Like a wet fisher tempest-tost,
Who sees throughout the weltering night
Afar on some low-lying coast
The streaming of a rainy light,
I saw this hour,—and now 'tis come;
The rooms are lit, the feast is set;
Within the twilight I am dumb,
My heart fill'd with a vague regret.

I cannot say, in Eastern style,
Where'er she treads the pansy blows;
Nor call her eyes twin-stars, her smile
A sunbeam, and her mouth a rose.
Nor can I, as your bridegrooms do,
Talk of my raptures. Oh, how sore

The fond romance of twenty-two
Is parodied ere thirty-four!

To-night I shake hands with the past,—
Familiar years, adieu, adieu!
An unknown door is open cast,
An empty future wide and new
Stands waiting. O ye naked rooms,
Void, desolate, without a charm,
Will Love's smile chase your lonely glooms,
And drape your walls, and make them warm

The man who knew, while he was young,
Some soft and soul-subduing air,
Melts when again he hears it sung,
Although 't is only half so fair.
So love I thee, and love is sweet
(My Florence, 't is the cruel truth)
Because it can to age repeat
That long-lost passion of my youth.

Oh, often did my spirit melt,
Blurred letters, o'er your artless rhymes!
Fair tress, in which the sunshine dwelt,
I've kissed thee many a million times!
And now 'tis done.—My passionate tears,
Mad pleadings with an iron fate,
And all the sweetness of my years,
Are blacken'd ashes in the grate.

Then ring in the wind, my wedding chimes;
Smile, villagers, at every door;
Old churchyard, stuff'd with buried crimes,
Be clad in sunshine o'er and o'er;
And youthful maidens, white and sweet,
Scatter your blossoms far and wide;
And with a bridal chorus greet
This happy bridegroom and his bride.

"This happy bridegroom!" there is sin
At bottom of my thankless mood:

What if desert alone could win
For me, life's chiefest grace and good?
Love gives itself; and if not given,
No genius, beauty, state, or wit,
No gold of earth, no gem of heaven,
Is rich enough to purchase it.

It may be, Florence, loving thee,
My heart will its old memories keep;
Like some worn sea-shell from the sea,
Fill'd with the music of the deep.
And you may watch, on nights of rain,
A shadow on my brow encroach;
Be startled by my sudden pain,
And tenderness of self-reproach.

It may be that your loving wiles
Will call a sigh from far-off years;
It may be that your happiest smiles
Will brim my eyes with hopeless tears;

It may be that my sleeping breath
Will shake, with painful visions wrung;
And, in the awful trance of death,
A stranger's name be on my tongue.

Ye phantoms, born of bitter blood,
Ye ghosts of passion, lean and worn,
Ye terrors of a lonely mood,
What do you here on a wedding morn?
For, as the dawning sweet and fast
Through all the heaven spreads and flows,
Within life's discord rude and vast,
Love's subtle music grows and grows.

And lighten'd is the heavy curse,
And clearer is the weary road;
The very worm the sea-weeds nurse
Is cared for by the Eternal God.
My love, pale blossom of the snow,
Has pierced earth wet with wintry showers,—

O may it drink the sun, and blow,
And be follow'd by all the year of flowers!

Black Bayard from the stable bring;
The rain is o'er, the wind is down,
Round stirring farms the birds will sing,
The dawn stand in the sleeping town,
Within an hour. This is her gate,
Her sodden roses droop in night,
And—emblem of my happy fate—
In one dear window there is light.

The dawn is oozing pale and cold
Through the damp east for many a mile;
When half my tale of life is told
Grim-featured Time begins to smile.
Last star of night that lingerest yet
In that long rift of rainy grey,
Gather thy wasted splendours, set,
And die into my wedding-day.

A BOY'S POEM.

A BOY'S POEM.

INTRODUCTION.

We have been parted now for twenty years;
Oft messages and gratulations kind
Have flown across the sea, and you have felt
A hand from England touch you 'neath the Palm;
At every little gift from you it seemed
As if my senses had been visited
By India's fragrant wind. With love like ours
These things are certain, as that in the spring
The rapture of the lark will fill the air,
The wind-flower light the woods. How strange will be
Our meeting, long expected, ere we die!
Both will be changed. The boat that forty years

Has heaved and laboured in the mounded brine,
Is cracked by sun-fire, bent by rainy squalls,
Eaten by restless foam. We will peruse
Each other's faces, read the matter there,
In our grim northern silence—and all be told
In one long passionate wring of claspèd hands.

You can remember how we, in our youth,
Looked forward to the years that were to come.—
We stood upon the verge of a great sea;
An airy rumour of its mighty capes,
Its isles of summer, its lone peaks of fire,
Unknown Americas that lay asleep,
Charmed our fond ears; forthwith we launched from shore,
The wind sang in the hollows of our sails,
And wonder rose on wonder as we went.
We now have voyaged many a foamy league,
Sailed far beyond the curtain of the sky
Which mocked our vision gazing from the strand.

Have we secured a haven of repose
Where we may moulder plank by plank in peace?
Or with our shrivelled canvas, battered hull,
Must we steer onward through the waste of waves,
Beneath the closing night?

The streams that burst,
Companions, from the misty mountain top,
And hear each other's music for a while,
Are far divided ere they meet the sea.
Shut from the blinding sun-bath of the noon
I see you stretched; the only living sound
Within the tingling silence of the heat,
The long wave's drowsy tumble on the bar;
And in your heart you hear another shore;
Then, like a charger by the trumpet pricked,
You start erect, a flash upon your face—
A spirt of smoke, the thunder of a gun,
A ship from England!

With much care and toil,
With something of the forethought of the squirrel

And labouring bee that ever works and sings,
I've laid up store, ere life became to me
Bare as a stubble-field. I've built a home
Beside the river which we used to love.
The murmur of the City reaches here,
And makes the silence more divinely still,
And the remembered turmoils of my youth
Sweeten this deep tranquillity of age.
If in a world that changes like a cloud,
A man may, in pure humbleness of heart,
Say he is happy, I am surely he.
Time unto me hath been the dearest friend;
For Time is like the peacefulness of grass,
Which clothes, as if with silence and deep sleep,
Deserted plains that once were loud with strife;
Which hides the marks of earthquake and of fire;
Which makes the rigid and the clay-cold grave
Smooth as a billow, tender with green light.
The world and I are friends. When I depart,
Upon the threshold I'll shake hands with Life

As with a generous and a cheerful host
Who gave me ample welcome 'neath his roof.
Now, in the sober evening of my days,
I do resemble in contentedness
An ancient grange half hid in harvest-home:
Though there is little warmth within my sky,
Though streaks of rain fall on the yellow woods,
Though wild winds clash my vanes — yet I have
stored
A summer's sunshine in my crowds of stacks;
Although hoar frost at morn is on the brier,
With oil, and roaring logs, I can make blithe
The long long winter night. I've suffered much,
And known the deepest sorrow man can know.
That pain has fled upon the troubled years:
Although the world is darker than before,
There is a pathos round the daisy's head;
The common sunshine in the common fields,
The runnel by the road, the clouds that grow
Out of the blue abysses of the air,

Do not as in my earlier days, oppress
Me with their beauty; for the grief that dims
The eye and cheek, hath touched them too, and made
Them dearer to me, being more akin.
Death weaves the subtle mystery of joy:
He gives a trembling preciousness to love,
Makes stern eyes dim above a sleeping face
Half-hidden in its cloud of golden curls.
Death is a greater poet far than Love;
The summer light is sweeter for his shade.

The past is very tender at my heart;
Full, as the memory of an ancient friend
When once again we stand beside his grave.
Raking amongst old papers thrown in haste
'Mid useless lumber, unawares I came
On a forgotten poem of my youth.
I went aside and read each faded page
Warm with dead passion, sweet with buried Junes,
Filled with the light of suns that are no more.

I stood like one who finds a golden tress
Given by loving hands no more on earth,
And starts, beholding how the dust of years,
Which dims all else, has never touched its light.
I stood before the grave-door of the past,
And to these eyes my yet unmouldered youth
Came forth like Lazarus. Thou swallow, Love,
Which thus revisit'st thine accustomed eaves,
Return, return to climes beyond the sea!
This ruined nest can never nurse thy young;
Thy twitter, and thy silver-flashing breast,
But mock me with the days that are no more.

I have been bold enough to send you this,
Though little of the Poet's shaping art
Is in these sheets, and nothing more was sought
Than that most sweet relief which dwells in verse
To a new spirit o'er which tyrannized,
Like a musician o'er an instrument,
The sights and sounds of the majestic world.

You knew me when my fond and ignorant youth
Was an unwindowed chamber of delight,
Deaf to all noise, sweet as a rose's heart:
A sudden earthquake rent it to the base,
And through the rifts of ruin sternly gleamed
An apparition of grey windy crag,
Black leagues of forest roaring like a sea,
And far lands dim with rain. *There* was my world
And place for evermore. When forth I went
I took my gods with me, and set them up
Within my foreign home. What love I had,
What admiration and keen sense of joy,
Unspent in verse, has been to me a stream
Feeding the roots of being; living sap
That dwelt within the myriad boughs of life,
And kept the leaves of feeling fresh and green.
Instead of sounding in the heads of fools,
Like wind within a ruin, it became
A pious benediction and a smile
On all the goings on of human life;

An incommunicable joy in day,
In lone waste places, and the light of stars.

Now as the years wear on, I hunger more
To see your face again before I die.
Last night I dreamed I saw a mighty ship
Through a great sea of moonlight bearing on,
Its coil of smoke dissolving into mist
Beyond its shining track ; and in my dream
I felt you on your way. May this be true !
Sometimes, in looking back upon my life,
I fear I have mistaken ill for good.
There are no children's voices in my house.
If I have never ventured from the strand,
Been spared the peril of the storm and rock,
I never have returned with merchandise.
I know that She has melted from your sight,
And that a colony of little graves
Makes that far earth as sacred as the sky.
Alone like me—your solitude is not

Empty like mine: lost faces come and go,
I have but thoughts. It may be that you weep,
But I have not a sorrow worth a tear:
Methinks to-night mine seems the harder fate.
The fire I kindled warmed myself alone,
And now, when it is sinking red and low
Within the solemn gloom, there is no hand
To heap on fuel. Therefore let it sink.
Life cannot bring me more than it has brought.
The oft-repeated tale has lost its charm.
I would not linger on to age, and have
The gold of life beat out to thinnest leaf.

Like winds that in the crimson autumn eves
Pipe of the winter snow, my prescient thoughts
Are touched with sadness. Ay, the leaf must fall
And rot in the long rain. The stage is bare,
The actor and the critic have retired,
And through the empty house a hand I know
Is putting out the lights; 'twill soon be dark.

PART I.

THERE was an awful silence in the house
Where my dead father lay. When years had passed,
That silence lay upon my mother's face,
And mingled with her motions and her speech.
We lived alone,—alone save one stern guest
Who sat beside our hearth and made it cold:
By many a hearth he sits. Yet never came
A murmur or complaint from her thin lips.

When but a trembling wind-flower of a child,
They set me in a large and crowded school.
The pale preceptor clad in rusty black,
The reading classes, and the murmuring forms
Were torture; and the ringing play-ground, hell.
I shrank from crowds of loud and boisterous boys.

The pain and forfeit of each game was mine ;
Contempt, and scorn, and taunts were rained on me ;
I wept within my little bed at night,
And wished that I were happy in my grave.
From out this depth of sorrow, slowly grew
A kindred and strange sympathy with eve,
With the unhoused and outcast winds, and with
The rain which I had heard so often weep
Alone, within the middle of the night,
Like a poor, beaten, and despisèd child
That has been thrust forth from its father's door.
And often when the burning sun went down,
I sat and wept unseen. The dark'ning earth,
The void deserted sky, were like myself;
They seemed unhappy, sad, forsaken things;
My childish sorrows made me kin with them;
Orphans we sat together. Sitting there,
What joy, when o'er the huddled chimney-tops
Rose the great yellow moon ! Since then I've seen
Her rise o'er mountain brows, droop large with bliss

O'er steaming autumn meads, touch lochs that spread
A hundred branching arms among the hills,
With leagues of throbbing silver—never more
With the delight of these remembered nights.

Tears dried upon my proud and burning cheeks;
When a tormentor struck me, to the soul
I stung him with a taunt. My new-found power
Made the world brighter; and to feel him wince
Was solitary joy—a fresh green turf
On which the caged lark sang. On autumn nights
My school-mates loved to gather at a forge,
And tell their stories round the furnace mouth.
I read strange legends in its crimson heart;
As I rehearsed the secrets of the fire,
I felt them grow toward me, drank the looks
They cast round to the dark and frowning night
That stood back from the glare. And these were they
Who hustled me at school, who drove me mad,
Who pelted me with names! The cowards shook,

And I smiled proudly in my secret heart:
I saw them tremble, and I struck them home.

Upon a day of wind and heavy rain
A crowd was huddling in the porch at school:
As I came up I heard a voice cry out,
"Ho, ho! here comes the lad that talks with ghosts
Sitting upon the graves." They laughed and jeered,
And gathered round me in a mocking ring,
And hurt me with their faces and their eyes.
With bitter words I smote them in my hate,
As with a weapon. A sudden blow, and wrath
Sprang upward like a flame. I struck, and blood,
Brighter than rubies, gleamed upon my hand;
And at the beauteous sight, from head to heel
A tiger's joy ran tingling through my veins,
And every finger hungered for a throat.
I burst the broken ring, and darted off
With my blood boiling, and my pulses mad.
I did not feel the rain upon my face;

With burning mouth I drank the cooling wind;—
And then, as if my limbs were touched by death,
A shudder shook me, all the rage that sprang
Like sudden fire in a deserted house
Making the windows fierce, had passed away;
And the cold rain beat heavy on me now;
The winds went through me.
                                        At the dead of night,
Fever beset me with a troop of fiends;
They hid in every crevice of the house
And called me with the voices of my mates,
And mocked me when I came. They made me blind,
And led me out to stumble among pits,
And smote me in my blackness. Oft they hung
Me o'er the edges of the dizzy steeps,
And laughed to see me swinging in the wind;
And then a blast would whirl me like a leaf,
From my frail hold out to the peopled air,
Where dark hands plucked at me and dragged me down.

I lay in darkness 'neath a weight of chains,—
A burst of day, and lo! a mighty sea
Of upturned faces murmured, heaved, and swayed
Around to see me die. Methought I fled
Along the road of death. Methought I heard
My mother calling from the life I left,
"Come back, come back, come back unto my love!"
"Whistle the 'scaped bird from the summer woods
Back to the spoiler's hand," I thought, and laughed,
And every cry grew fainter as I ran.
I paused upon a drear bewildered road,
Lined with dark trees, or ghosts, which only seemed
A darker gloom in gloom, and, far away,
A glare went up as of a sunken fire.
"This is the land of death, and that is hell,"
I cried, as I went on toward the glare.
I climbed a bank of gloom, and there I saw
A burning sea upon a burning shore,
A lone man sitting black against the light,
His long black shadow stretching o'er the sands,

Long as earth's sunset shades. Then all at once,
Like landscapes in the red heart of a fire,
The vision crumbled, and methought I stood
Beside an ancient and unused canal,
Choked with great stems and monstrous leaves, and filled
With olive-coloured water thick as oil.
All here and there 'twas patched and skinned with green,
The cream of idle years. Upon the green,
There blushed and glowed a dewy crimson rose,—
Some hand had thrown it scarce an hour ago.
I hurried on, that I might overtake
Whoe'er had passed that way. I stood in fear—
As a stream flows for ever past a tree,
A line of sable shapes came winding by
With downcast eyes and cloaked from head to foot.
Methought I stood for weeks, and months, and years,
And still the shapes came past. My horror grew
Until I burst the silence with a cry ;

Then, as a trail of smoke is torn by winds,
The long line wavered, broke, and disappeared.

At length, amid the phantoms of my brain,
A kind white face was mixed. It came and went.
Sometimes it slowly stole across the gloom,
And paused to gaze on me, then died away;
And sometimes it would lean above my couch,
And look into my eyes. As once it came
And hung above me for a silent hour,
I raised my wasted hand and touched its cheek:
It did not frown on me;—next, bolder grown,
I wandered o'er its brow, its mouth, its hair,
And then methought it smiled. I shrunk in fear,
Then touched the cheek again; and, wondering, said,
"Surely this should be my own mother's face!"
And dimly felt as if enclosed in arms,
As if an eager mouth were pressed to mine.
Delirium slid from off me like the flood

From off the world, and slowly I awoke
To the full knowledge of my mother's love,—
"God hath returned thee from the gates of death,
My poor tormented child!" That hour of joy!
That welcome back to life! I was as one
Drawn sorely wounded from his bed of blood
'Mong the war-horse's hoofs; as one redeemed
From the sea's foamy mouth, or arms of fire.
And in the progress of the weary days
My mother sat beside my bed, and told
How the long battle swayed 'tween life and death;
And how she 'tended me, and how, one night,
The life was wavering 'tween my parted lips,
Loose as the film that flutters on the grate;
And how, at twelve, she thought that all was o'er.
I stood within the street one April day,
Wan as a healthless primrose, which a leaf
Had shaded, that it could not drink the sun.
I lay down on a night of stormy rain;
The snow had fallen, and the world was dumb.

Now, showers of melody from unseen larks
Fell the long day upon the golden fields,
And the bare woods were putting on their green.

In those dark days I was surprised with joy
The deepest I have found upon the earth.
One night, when my weak limbs were drawing
strength
From meats and drinks, and long delicious sleep,
I raised a book to kill the tedious hours—
The glorious Dreamer's—he, whose walls enclosed
An emperor's state; upon whose lonely sleep
The secret heavens opened, peopled thick
With angels, as the beam with swirling motes.
I was like one who at his girdle wears
An idle key, and with it, purposeless,
In the mere impulse of a wayward mood,
Opes a familiar door, and stands amazed,
Blind with the prisoned splendour which escapes,
Filling his dusky home. From earth's rude noise

I wandered through the quiet land of thought,
Where all was peaceful as the happy fields
Wherein the shades are silent with deep bliss,
And not a sound doth jar the golden air.
For me no more existed space or time,
Nor in my narrow being did I live;
That miser Death, whose lean and covetous hand
Hoards up the pomps and glories of the world,
Gave up his treasures, and Experience
Was like a fenceless common over which
I ranged at will. And so I have the noise
Of armies round me, wear the monarch's crown,
Die in the martyr's fire. Whatever joy
Or sorrow man has tasted, that I share;
Nor can my life be measured by my years.

The summer had been cold, the harvest wet,
And the reaped corn lay rotting in the fields.
Men who at morning stood as prosperous
As bearded autumn, were, ere sunset, poor

As a worn scarecrow fluttering dingy rags
Within the feeble wind. Each month, the boom
Of a great battle travelled on the wind,
Smiting the hearers pale. Down came the snow.
'Tis said, the blown and desperate forester
Chased by a lean and hunger-pinched bear,
Drops, one by one, his garments in his flight,
To make the monster pause—In those dark months,
My weary mother, chased by poverty,
Gave, one by one, her treasures—precious things
Hallowed by love and death; yet all in vain:
The terror followed on our flying heels.
So, on a summer morning, I was led
Into a square of warehouses, and left
'Mong faces merciless as engine-wheels.—
The right hand learns its cunning, and the feet
That tread upon the rough ways of the world
Grow mercifully callous. Months crept past;
If they brought bitterness, why then complain?
Will Fate relax his stern and iron brows

For a boy's foolish tears? In this grim world,
The beggar tosses on his straw, the king
Upon his velvet bed. Yet a few steps,
And Death will lift the load the heavens gave
From off the burdened back. I now can look
Upon those distant years with calmer eyes
And melancholy pleasure. Then it was
Love oped the dusky volume of my life,
And wrote, with his own hot and hurrying hand,
A chapter in fierce splendours. Then it was
I built an altar—raised a flame to Love;
And a strong whirlwind threw the altar down,
And strewed its sparks on darkness.

In a room,
Quiet, 'mid that building full of groaning wheels,
She sat, and sang as merry as a lark
Whose cage is shining in the sunny beam;
Laughed, like a happy fountain in a cave
Brightening the gloomy rocks. O'er costly gauze
Her busy twinkling fingers moved,—like Spring's,

Flowers grew beneath their touch. How I began
To love her first is now to me unknown
As how I came from nothingness to life.
Her frequent duties led her through our room ;
I thrilled, when through the noises of the day
I caught her door, the rustle of her dress,
Her coming footstep. Oh ! that little foot
Did more imperiously stir my blood
Than the heart-shaking trumpets of a king
Heard through the rolling, ever-deepening shout,
When houses, peopled to the chimney-tops,
Lean forward, eager for the coming sight.
She flew across our room with sudden gleam,
Like bird of Paradise. Sometimes she paused,
And tossed amongst us a few crumbs of speech,
Or pelted us in sport with saucy words,
Then vanished, like a star into a cloud.
Love's magic finger touched my ear and eye ;
And music, which before was but a sound,
Now something far more passionate than myself

Spake trembling of her beauty; and the world
Folded around me fragrant as a rose.

'T was prime of May; and every square became
A murmuring camp of Summer. Now and then
A dizzy and bewildered butterfly
Fluttered through noisy streets. A week was mine,
To wander uncontrolled as cloud or breeze.
The eve before I went, there came a thirst
Upon me for her presence. Long I stood,
My hand upon her door, my fearful heart
Loud in my ears. I heard her sweet "Come in,"
And entered. She was standing in the light,
Upgathering, in the bondage of the comb,
Her glorious waves of hair. She welcomed me
With dazzling laughter:—"Oh, I'm glad you've come!
See this rich present sleeping in its folds!
Do tell me how I look." The crimson scarf
She wreathed around her shoulders and her head,
Till her sweet face was set and framed in silk;

And then, a very sunbeam in my eyes,
She stood and smiled; soon with a sullen lip
She stripped the glowing silk from neck and head,
And threw it down; then clapped her tiny hands,
And, round me standing in a marsh of doubt,
She danced like elfin fire. "In dream" (I spoke,
Bewildered by her sunshine and her shade)
"I saw a rose of such a breadth and glow,
It seemed as it had sucked into its heart
All fragrance, sun, and colour, and had left
Its poor defrauded sisterhood to hang
Their pale heads scentless in the careless wind;
But ere, with happy hand, I plucked the rose—
A summer in itself—and brought it thee,
I woke to barren midnight." "Bah!" She turned,
And froze my speech to silence with a look.
"In dreamland you have very vast estates,
Not worth an ear of corn." At her disdain
Laughing outright, I said, "The scornful flag
That flouts by day and night besieging foes,

Falls in their hands. I came to say good-bye."
"Well."
"I leave the city for some days; and thought
That you might like—"
"What?"
"To see me ere I went."

"I wish to Heaven that Harry, Charles, and you,
Would go and ne'er return. I'm sure your backs
Are fairer than your faces."
"Poor little god!
Weary of incense; most unhappy rose,
Plagued with enamoured bees—too innocent
To blame its own sweet breath! A lover slay,
And hang him up within your beauty's field,
As the gruff husbandman hangs up a crow
To warn his brethren off."
The sunlight flashed
Into her face. She heaved a little sigh,
And dropped her eyelids down upon her cheek,

Though all the while the rogues laughed 'neath their
shades,
And a smile played and flickered round the mouth
So rosily demure.
"'Twere little use.
'T is very hard to know which way to turn.
A lover is as stupid as the fish
That, with a broken barb within its gills,
Leaps at another bait. Where are you going?"

"Down the long river, past the fortressed rock
To that fair island in the sparkling sea,
Across whose face through all the scented hours
Change melts in finer change, from clear green light
To purple thunder-gloom. She's courted too—
For when she smiles the proud and dimpled sea
Fawns on her fringe of flowers; and when she frowns,
Gone are his flickering waves and miles of light,
Grey is his only wear."
"And when return?"

" On Saturday."

" I'll look for flowers. Could not
You come on Friday ?"

" Wherefore do you ask ?"

" Oh, nothing, nothing ; but I know you will.
Now won't you say you 'll come ?"

" And my reward ?"

" Ah, must I buy your favours ? Then I'll let
You place the fairest rose of all your wreath
Amid my hair."

" Where it will deeper glow
With pride, than when it sat upon its stem,
And drank ambrosial air."

" Thou mocker !"

As I went,
She laughed and called me back.—" *True* flowers, you know ;
Not those pale moonlight things that grow so thick

In gardens of your dreams; which might be given
By ghost to ghost, in some serene farewell,
For a love-token and remembrancer
To look on in the shades. True flowers I want
To blush in mortal hair." I left her light,
As happy as a serf who leaves his king
Ennobled, and possessed of broader lands
Than the great rain-cloud trailing from the fens
Can blacken with his shadow.

PART II.

THE morn rose blue and glorious o'er the world;
The steamer left the black and oozy wharves,
And floated down between dark ranks of masts.
We heard the swarming streets, the noisy mills;
Saw sooty foundries full of glare and gloom,
Great bellied chimneys tipped by tongues of flame,
Quiver in smoky heat. We slowly passed
Loud building-yards, where every slip contained
A mighty vessel with a hundred men
Battering its iron sides. A cheer! a ship
In a gay flutter of innumerous flags
Slid gaily to her home. At length the stream
Broadened 'tween banks of daisies, and afar
The shadows flew upon the sunny hills;
And down the river, 'gainst the pale blue sky,

A town sat in its smoke. Look backward now!
Distance has stilled three hundred thousand hearts,
Drowned the loud roar of commerce, changed the proud
Metropolis which turns all things to gold,
To a thick vapour o'er which stands a staff
With smoky pennon streaming on the air.
Blotting the azure too, we floated on,
Leaving a long and weltering wake behind.
And now the grand and solitary hills
That never knew the toil and stress of man,
Dappled with sun and cloud, rose far away.
My heart stood up to greet the distant land
Within the hollows of whose mountains lochs
Moan in their restless sleep; around whose peaks,
And craggy islands ever dim with rain,
The lonely eagle flies. The ample stream
Widened into a sea. The boundless day
Was full of sunshine and divinest light,
And far above the region of the wind
The barred and rippled cirrus slept serene,

With combed and winnowed streaks of faintest cloud
Melting into the blue. A sudden veil
Of rain dimmed all; and when the shade drew off,
Before us, out toward the mighty sun,
The firth was throbbing with glad flakes of light.
The mountains from their solitary pines
Ran down in bleating pastures to the sea;
And round and round the yellow coasts I saw
Each curve and bend of the delightful shore
Hemmed with a line of villas white as foam.
Far off, the village smiled amid the light;
And on the level sands, the merriest troops
Of children sported with the laughing waves,
The sunshine glancing on their naked limbs.
White cottages, half smothered in rose blooms,
Peeped at us as we passed. We reached the pier,
Whence girls in fluttering dresses, shady hats,
Smiled rosy welcome. An impatient roar
Of hasty steam; from the broad paddles rushed
A flood of pale green foam, that hissed and freathed

Ere it subsided in the quiet sea.
With a glad foot I leapt upon the shore,
And, as I went, the frank and lavish winds
Told me about the lilac's mass of bloom,
The slim laburnum showering golden tears,
The roses of the gardens where they played.

At eve I lay in utter indolence
Upon a crag's high heather-purpled head.
The sun hung o'er a sea of wrinkled gold,
And o'er him fleecy vapour, rack of cloud,
And thin suspended mists hung tremulous
In fiery ecstasy; while high in heaven,
Discerned afar between the crimson streaks,
And melting away toward the lucid east,
Like clouds of cherubs tiny cloudlets slept
In soft and tender rose. When I returned,
The air was heavy with the breath of flowers,
And from the houses of the rich there came
Low-breathing music through the balmy gloom:

Linked lovers passed me, lost in murmurous talk :
That fragrant night of happiness and love
My soul closed o'er its secret like a rose
That sates itself with its own heart of bliss.
That fragrant night of happiness and love
She seemed to lie within my heart and smile.
The village lights were sprinkled on the hill ;
And on the dim and solitary loch,
Our oar-blades stirred the sea to phantom light,
A hoary track ran glimmering from the keel.
Like scattered embers of a dying fire,
The village lights had burnt out one by one ;
I lay awake, and heard at intervals
A drowsy wave break helpless on the shore,
Trailing the rattling pebbles as it washed
Back to the heaving gloom. "Come, blessed Sleep,
And with thy fingers of forgetfulness
Tie up my senses till the day we meet,
And kill this gap of time." By sweet degrees
My slumberous being closed its weary leaves

In drowsy bliss, and slowly sank in dream,
As sinks the water-lily 'neath the wave.

Next morning I rose early and looked forth:
The quiet sky was veiled with dewy haze;
Beneath it slept the dull and beamless sea;
The flowers hung dim and sodden in the dew;
Strange birds fed in the walks, and one unseen
Sang from the apple-tree. I dressed in haste;
And when the proud sun fired the dripping pines,
I wandered forth, and drank with thirsty eyes
The coolness of the sun-illumined brooks
In which the quick trout played. The speckless light,
The beauty of the morning, drew me on
Into a gloomy glen. The heavy mists
Crept up the mountain sides; I heard the streams;
The place was saddened with the bleat of sheep.
"'Tis surely in such lonely scenes as these,
Mythologies are bred. The rolling storms—
The mountains standing black in mist and rain,

With long white lines of torrents down their sides—
The ominous thunder creeping up the sky—
The homeless voices at the dead of night
Wandering among the glens—the ghost-like clouds
Stealing beneath the moon—are but as stuff
Whence the awe-stricken herdsman could create
Gods for his worship." Then, as from a cup,
Morn spilt warm sunshine down the mountain-side.
Cuckoo! cuckoo! woke somewhere in the light;
I started at the sound, and cried, "O Voice!
I've heard you often in the poet's page—
Now, in your stony wilds—and I have read
Of white arms clinging round a sentenced neck
Upon a morn of death; of bitter wrong
Freezing sweet love to hate; of fond ambition
Which plaits and wears a wretched crown of straw,
And dreams itself a king; of inward shame,
To which a lingering and long-drawn death
Were bed of roses, incense, and a smile.
With anxious heart I hear my distant hours

Gather like far-off thunder. Canst thou tell
What things await me on my road of life
As did your floating voice?" Behold the sea!
Far flash its glittering leagues, and 'neath the sun
There gleams from coast to coast a narrow line
Of blinding and intolerable light.
I lay beneath a glimmering sycamore
Drowsy with murmuring bees.—As o'er my limbs
There palpitated countless lights and shades,
I heard the quiet music of the waves,
And saw the great hills standing dim in heat.

At height of noon a gloomy fleece of rain
Was hanging o'er the zenith. On it crept,
Drinking the sunlight from a hundred glens;
Blackening hill by hill; smiting the sea's
Bright face to deadly pallor; till at last
It drowned the world from verge to verge in gloom.
A sky-wide blinding glare—the thunder burst—
Again heaven opened in a gape of flame;

Heavy as lead came down the loosened rain—
I heard it hissing in the smoking sea;
It slackened soon, the sun blazed through, and then
The fragment of a rainbow in the gloom
Burned on the rainy sea—a full-sail'd ship
Apparent stood within the glorious light
From hull to highest spar. The tempest trailed
His shadowy length across the distant hills:
The birds from hiding-places came and sang,
And ocean laughed for miles beneath the sun.

I and my cousins started in the morn
To wander o'er the mountains and the moors.
How different from the hot and stony streets!
The dark red springy turf was 'neath our feet,
Our walls the blue horizon, and our roof
The boundless sky; a perfect summer-day
We walked 'mid unaccustomed sights and sounds;
Fair apparitions of the elements
That lived a moment on the air, then passed

To the eternal world of memory.
O'er rude unthrifty wastes we held our way
Whence never lark rose upward with a song,
Where no flower lit the marsh : the only sights,
The passage of a cloud—a thin blue smoke
Far on the idle heath—now caught, now lost,
The pink road wavering to the distant sky.
At noon we rested near a mighty hill,
That from our morning hut slept far away
Azure and soft as air. Upon its sides
The shepherds shouted 'mid a noise of dogs ;
A stream of sheep came slowly trickling down,
Spread to a pool, then poured itself in haste.
The sun sunk o'er a crimson fringe of hills :
The violet evening filled the lower plain,
From which it upward crept and quenched the lights—
Awhile the last peak burned in lingering rose,
And then went out. We toiled at dead of night
Through a deep glen, the while the lonely stars
Trembled above the ridges of the hills ;

And in the utter hush the ear was filled
With low sweet voices of a thousand streams,
Some near, some far remote—faint trickling sounds
That dwelt in the great solitude of night
Upon the edge of silence. A sinking moon
Hung on one side and filled the shattered place
With gulfs of gloom, with floating shades, and threw
A ghostly glimmer on wet rock and pool.

Then came a day of deep and blissful peace,
In which familiar thoughts and images
By which we know and recognise ourselves
Fell from me, and I felt as new and strange
As a free spirit which has shaken off
The wrappings of this life. Upon a stair,
The remnant of the tower, I sat and watched
Tumultuous piles of cloud upon the hills,
The sea-mew sweeping silent as a dream,
The black rocks ringed with white, the creeping sail,
The wandering greens and purples of the sea.

We heard the people singing in the hay,
A single girl-voice leading, all the field
Bursting in chorus ; a little off, the Laird,
Upon his shaggy pony of the isles,
Drew rein and heard the legend of his house.
At eventime the mighty barn was cleared,
The torches lit, the lads and lasses came,
And to the yelling pipes, in loop and chain,
And whirling circles, spun the maddened reels.

Tradition murmured of a sullen lake
Imprisoned in the solitary hills
Far off. We talked of it around the fire,
Arranged our plans, and with the rising sun
Our boat was half-way o'er the narrow loch.
How pure the morning on the tremulous deep!
Far to the east two crimson islands burned
Like pointed flames. The sea was clad with birds,
The air was resonant with mingled cries,
And oft a dark and glutted cormorant

Flapped 'cross our path. As silent as a ghost
A whale arose and sunned his glistening sides,
Then sank as still. We hung above the bow,
And through the pale green water clear as air,
The mighty army of the herrings passed
In silvery flash on flash. The glorious main
That flowed and dimpled round the morning isles,
Laughed with as huge a joy as on that morn
When God said to it, "Live!"

The gloomy lake,
Unvisited by sunbeam or by breeze,
Slept on the ruined shore. High up in heaven,
Rose splintered summits, visited alone
By the loud blackness of the drowning storms,
The momentary meteors of the air,
The solitary stars on windless nights,
Sailing across the chasms: there they stood
In stony silence in the sunny noon,
Crushed by the tread of earthquake, split by fire,
Horrid with grisly clefts in which the Spring

Dared never laugh in green. A weary cloud,
Half down, had lost its way; an eagle hung,
A black speck in the sun. We raised a shout,
A sullen echo—then were heard the sweet
And skiey tones of spirits 'mid the peaks,
Faint voice to faint voice shouting; dim halloos
From unseen cliff and ledge; and answers came
From some remoter region far withdrawn
Within the pale blue sky.
On our return,
Upon a shoulder of the mountain streamed
The sun's last gush of gold: above our heads
The arch of heaven blushed with rippled rose
Back to the gates of morning, and beneath,
Each lazy undulation of the deep
Changed like a pigeon's neck. Afar, the house
Sat like a white shell on the low green shore,
And storm-worn cliffs, though inland many a mile,
Came out above its head. As on we sailed,
And as the azure night, which gathered fast

In glen and hollow, cooled the burning sky,
Stole the sleek splendour from the indolent wave,
Drew o'er the world a veil of dewy grey,
The boatmen sang the music of the land;
And, in its sad and low monotony,
There lived the desolation of the waste,
The bitter outcry of the sweeping blast,
The sob of ocean round the iron shores.

Next morning we came early 'cross the moors,
And reached again the village by the sea.

There was a ruined chapel on the coast,
And by it lay a little grassy grave
Still as a couching lamb. The people told
How years ago, a grey-haired, childless man,
(His name is still remembered by the world,)
Came to these shores, and lay down there to rest
Till the last trumpet's cry. Near it I sat
On my last afternoon; and while the wind
Chequered my page with shadows of the grass,

I wrote this love-song sitting by the grave,
Nor smiled to think that so ran on the world.

"Mary, Mary, sweetest name!
Linked with many a poet's fame.
A Mary, with meek eyes of blue,
And low sweet answers, gently drew
The weary Christ to Bethany,
When no home on earth had He.

"When first I saw your tender face,
Saw you, loved you from afar,
My soul was like forlornest space
Made sudden happy by a star.
I heard the lark go up to meet the dawn,
The sun is sinking in the splendid sea;
Through this long day hast thou had one, but one
Poor thought of me?

"O happiest of isles!
In every garden blows

The large voluptuous-bosomed rose
For musky miles and miles.
I wander round this garden coast;
I see the glad blue waters run;
In the light of Thy beauty I am lost,
As the lark is lost in the sun.

"O heart! 'twas thine own happiness that gave
The beauty which has been upon the earth,
The glory stretching from day's golden birth
Unto his crimson grave.
From thee is every sight;
From thee the splendour of the firth,
The banquet of the morning light.

"Yet, Love, thy very happiness alarms!
To be beloved is something so divine,
I dare not hope it can be mine.
My heart is stirring like a nest with young—
I know that many and many a former brood

Were robbed by cruel fate, and never sung
  Within a summer wood.
Something forbodes me pain ;
  The image of my fear—
A maypole standing in the mocking rain
  With garlands torn and sere!

" To-day I chanced to pass
A churchyard covered with forgetful grass ;
And as one puts the hair from off a face,
  I put aside the grass ; and, on the stones,
  Saw roses wreathing bones:
And, in the rankest corner of the place,
Set in a ghastly scroll of skulls and flowers,
And belts of serpents twined and curled,
  I traced a crowned and mantled Death,
Asleep upon a World.
How grim the carver's style—
  The tarnished coffins, rotten palls,
  The weeping of the charnel walls,—

When one is lord of happy hours,
  When one is breathing priceless breath—
Made happy by a smile!

"The sheep they leap in golden parks;
  My blood is bliss, my heart is pleasure;
Then let my song flow like a lark's
  Above his nested treasure.
What care I for the circling cup?
  What care I for applausive breath?
For the stern secret folded up
  In the closed hand of Death?
Bring me Love's honied nightshade; fill it high;
  I know its madness, all its wild deceit;
I know the anguish of the morning sky
  When brain and eyeballs beat.
I cannot throw it down and fly—
  The poison is so sweet
That I must drink and drink, although I die."

The thought of the to-morrow was a goad
That urged me forth along the lonely shore:
Alone I wandered through the breathless gloom,
Feeding upon the honey of my heart
With a strange thrill of fear. While on I walked,
As if the sea would fain delay my steps,
Out of the darkness rushed a ghostly fringe
Wailing, and licked my feet, and then withdrew.
What wouldst thou with me, melancholy one?
What prophecy is in thy voice to-night?
What evil dost thou 'bode? Then, o'er my head,
To a low breathing wind the darkness cracked,
Rolled to a crescent shore of vapour, washed
By a blue bay of midnight keen with stars.
The moon came late, and quivered on the waves;
And, far away, 'tween dim horizons, beds
Of restless silver shifted on the sea.
Home by the margin of the deep I went,
And sought repose; and all the night a surge
Mourned bodefully around the shores of sleep.

I plucked my flowers before the dawn. I heard
A loud bell ringing on the dewy pier,
And went on board. Away the vessel sped,
Leaving a foamy track upon the sea,
A smoky trail in air. We touched, half-way,
A melancholy town, that sat and pined
'Mong weedy docks and quays. Thence went the train;
It shook the sunny suburbs with a scream;
Skimmed milk-white orchards, walls and mossy trees
One sheet of blossom; flew through living rocks,
Adown whose maimed and patient faces, tears
Trickle for ever; plunged in howling gloom;
Burst into blinding day; afar was seen
The river gleaming 'gainst a wall of rain,
A moment and no more; for suddenly
Upflew the envious and earthen banks,
And shut all out, until the engine slacked.
Amid the fiery forges and the smoke
I reached the warehouse. At the accustomed hour
Of rest at noon I stole toward her room;

I listened, but I could not hear a sound
For my loud-beating heart. With troubled hand,
I rested on the door, which stood, like death,
Between my soul and bliss. It oped at last
On a bare room that struck me with a chill.
I came back to my task; I dared not ask
A casual question; for I feared each one,
By only turning on me his calm eyes,
Would read my secret.
On that afternoon,
I bore a message to the upper flats:
When I returned, the stairs were black as night:
I heard two girls come slowly up the steps,
Bearing their water-loads: they laid them down,
And thus I heard them talking in the dark.

"Again to work so late! The second time
We have been treated so within the month,
And now the nights are fine. I hate that wretch,
Stealing up-stairs in india-rubber shoes,

Creeping from room to room, till, ere you know,
He is beside you; in each corner poking
With his white weasel face. He cooks his meals
Within his empty house; his sole companion,
A wretched cat that on his bounty starves—
A shadow, like himself."

"His brother, too,
The upper and the nether millstone they,
And we are ground between. Last pay, because
I was one morning some ten minutes late
(Aunt Martha had been more than usual ill)—
He mulct me of an hour—a glass of port,
To redden in his nose! As there he sat,
Steaming from dinner, and struck off the pence,
If I had only pricked him with my needle,
Old Red-gills had bled wine."

"Both the same stuff.
We are the bees that labour in the hive;
They eat the honey. At this very hour,
Mary will ope the ball. Would I were there!

To-night she wears the scarf that Morris gave.
How fond she seems of him!"

"At dinner-time,
She bade me come and see her in her dress.
Joy stood like candles in her mother's eyes.
She rose up in her robe of snowy lace,
Her coal-black hair, which all the men admire,
Rolled up with pearls, and looked, by all the world,
Like a white waterfall. Each thing she wore,
From her rich head-dress to her satin foot,
Was given to her by him. She said she meant
To dress her head with living flowers;—what fun,
To use the roses, by one lover brought,
To turn the other's brain!"

"What is he like?"

"As yellow as a guinea. Rich, she says;
His father died abroad. He is so mad,
I verily believe, to please a whim,
He'd deck her out in richest cloth of gold,

And slipper her with silver."

"I only hope

That all may prove as pleasant as it seems.
I wish I were among them standing up,
To glide off to the music.—Something stirs!"

"Let us slip in."

Hope's door closed with a clang. * * I rose up calm,
Calm as a country when the storm is o'er,
And broken boughs are hanging from the trees,
And swollen streams have crept within their banks,
Leaving a mighty marge of wreck and sand
Along the soppy fields. When I went home,
My mother dwelling in the empty house
With sorrow for a husband, like reproach
Struck through my selfish rage. She crept to bed,
And, from the barren desert of the night,
Prayer, like a choir of angels, bore her up
To heaven, where she talked alone with God.

I ground between my teeth, " The day has come
That progressed like a monarch with his court;
Of whose approach each courier hour that passed,
Brought sweetest tidings, like gay winds that sing
In the delighted ears of sunny May,
Sitting among the golden buttercups.
'June, drowned with roses, comes;' to which my thoughts
Arose, as from the earth a thousand larks,
In salutation to the dawn. And now
I sit degraded. Palaces of dream
Shivered around; uncounted wealth that stuffed,
This morn, the coffers of my heart, all false
And base as forgers' coin.

" A merchant with his fortune on the deep—
A mother with her brave and precious boy
Flung where the wave of battle breaks in death—
Ventures no more than we do when we love.
What sweet enchantments hover round Love's name!

Far out to sea, from off her syren isles,
Steal wandering melodies, and lie in wait
To lure the sailor to her fatal shores
Within the crimson sunset. 'T is our doom
To sit unhappy in the round of self.
From our necessities of love arise
Our keenest heartaches and our miseries.
When death and change are flying in the sky,
Our spirits tremble like a nest of doves,
Beneath the falcon's wing. Each time we love,
We turn a nearer and a broader mark
To that keen archer, Sorrow, and he strikes.
O that the heart could, like a housewife, sit
By its own fire, and let the world go by
Unheeded as the stream before the door!
Love cannot look upon a dingy cloud,
But straightway there's a rainbow; and we walk
Blind with a fond delusion in our eyes,
Which paints each grey crag, rose. Whene'er we meet
A giddy girl—a mountain beck that sings

And sparkles from its shallowness, ourselves
Its glorifying sun,—her heart an inn,
Or caravanserai amid the sands,
With new guests every night,—to Love she gleams
A daughter of the dawn. She flings, in sport,
The jewel of our happiness away:
To her,—each bubble blown by Idleness,
Lolling with peacock's feather in the sun,
An ever-radiant wonder,—nought. To us,
The change between bright Spring's exuberant lark,
And Autumn's shy and solitary bird;
Instead of dancing to our graves in sheen,
Walking in sober grey.

"A growing wind
Flutters my sails, and my impatient prow
Is plunging like a fiery steed reined in;
It hears the glee of billows. Blow, thou wind,
And let me out upon my seething way,
Crushing the waves to foam! My cooped-up life
Is pained by fulness, and would seek relief

In reckless effort. When the heart is jarred,
'T is vain to sit and feed a slothful grief;
Out of ourselves, as an infected house,
We come; then Nature heals—she is our guide.
By her eternal dial, which keeps time
With the invariable and dread advance
Of midnight's starry armies, must we set
Our foolish wandering hours. Each child believes,
That, by the burning nettle, ever grows
A cool assuaging leaf. Faith, fair and true—
A man is stung by sorrow, and his cure
Is the next man he meets. By simple love,
He sits down at his feast, tastes all his joys,
Yet leaves him none the less.

"Love, unreturned,
Hath gracious uses; the keen pang departs,
The sweetness never. Sorrow's touch doth ope
A mingled fount of sweet and bitter tears,
No summer's heat can dry, no winter's cold
Lock up in ice. When music grieves, the past

Returns in tears. The red and setting sun
Is beauty indescribable, and leads
The heart 'mong graves. The old man shuts the door
Of his still soul, and, in the inmost room,
Sits days with memory. Grey Adam, roofed
With smoky rafters—how unlike the blue
That bent o'er Eden !—forgets Eve's faded face—
His wandering boy—his eyes are far away ;
And, in his heart, remembrance sad and sweet,
Of Paradise long lost.

" As a wild mother, when her child is dead,
Flings herself down on the unheeding face,
And pours more passionate kisses on the lips
Than when they kissed again, and then starts up,
And, in a dreamy luxury of grief,
Strews the white corse with flowers :—' I'll lay thee out,
My poor dead love, and fondlier gaze on thee,
Than when thou smiled amid thy golden hair,
And sang more sweet than Hope. No tears ; for Death

Saw thee when loveliest, and his icy touch
Preserves thy look for ever. It is well:
The only things that change not are the dead.
Now thou art safe from Time's defacing hand,
From staling custom, and, sadder far than all,
From human fickleness. In after years,
It might be, I would scarce have followed thee,
A mourner to thy grave. Thou art so fair,
That, gazing on thee, clamorous grief becomes
For very reverence, mute. If mighty Death
Made our rude human faces by his touch
Divinely fair as thine, O, never more
Would strong hearts break o'er biers. There sleeps to-night
A sacred sweetness on thy silent lips,
A solemn light upon thine ample brow,
That I can never, never hope to find
Upon a living face. Within thy grave
I'll lay thee; and above will memory hang
An ever-mourning willow!'"

PART III.

A DARK hour came, and left us desolate :
Then, as a beggar thrust by menial hands
From comfortable doors, doth wrap his rags
Around him, ere he face the whistling wind
And flying showers that travel through the night,
We gathered what we had ; and she and I
Went forth together to the cruel world.
O we were bare and naked as the trees
That stand up silent in the freezing air,
With black boughs motionless against the sky,
While midnight holds her lonely starry sway.

We crept into a half-forgotten street
Of frail and tumbling houses propt by beams,
And ruined courts which, centuries before,

Rung oft to iron heels,—which palfreys pawed,
As down the mighty steps the Lady came
Bright as the summer morning,—peopled now
By outcasts, sullen men, bold girls who sat
Pounding sand in the sun. The day we came
The windows from which beauty leant and smiled,
Were stuffed with rags, or held a withered stick
Whence foul clothes hung to dry. Beneath an arch
Two long-haired women fought; while high above,
Heads thrust through broken panes, two shrill-voiced crones
Scolded each other. Hell-fire burst at night
Through the thin rind of earth; the place was loud
With drunken strife, hoarse curses; then the cry
Of a lost woman by a ruffian felled
Made the blood stop. Ah! different from the dream
That keeps my memory fragrant—sunny air,
Stirred into drowsy music by the bees;
Hollyhocks glowing at the open door;
A dark, grave, loving face; a step and voice

That faded in that time! We dwelt alone:
Red Autumn died unseen along the waste,
The soundless snow came down in thickening flakes,
And Poverty, who sat beside our hearth,
Blew out the feeble fire, and all was dark.

It was the closing evening of the year,
The night that I was born. I laughed, and said,
" The old year brought me in his dying arms,
And laid me in your breast; his last task done,
He went away through whirls of blinding snow."
She murmured, " 'T is the first time in these years
We cannot hold your birth-night as our wont,
With feast, and smiling friends, and quiet mirth
O'er-shadowed by the memory of the dead
Until 'tis almost sad. 'T is sixteen years,
And every night I've looked upon your sleep
Although you knew it not. Of those who were
Dear to me on the night that you were born,
You only now remain." I knew her thoughts,

" *He* wearies for us in the happy fields ;
His bliss is incomplete till we are there."
My mother spoke with heart far, far away.
" I count the years, as eagerly as one
Long separated from the friends he loves
Counts the slow milestones as he travels home.
Your life is all before you with its joy;
The only thing I covet is the grave."
She kissed me, put her withered hand in mine.
Its touch brought tears. I thought of all the pain,
The sorrow which had grown up in her life
Through her long years of widowhood, like grass
In a deserted street. Then all at once
A hundred church-bells struck the hour of twelve ;
A mighty shout went up, " The year is dead!"
There were glad footsteps on a thousand stairs,
And happy greetings in a thousand homes ;
None said, God bless us. Bitterly I cried,
" What great unpardoned sin is on our race
That we are so accursed ? Where'er we go,

Calamity glides ever in our track,
A ghost implacable. Were I to die
On this great night when Christendom is glad,
I would be all unpitied and unknown,
As a forgotten captive, or a worm
That dies unheard of underneath the ground."
But she reproached me with her silent eyes.

The sun burst forth ; 'neath sheltering cliff and bank
Lay melting wreaths, which, in its swift retreat,
The army of the snow had left. Whene'er
The gloomy Winter round him called his showers,
Legions of howling winds, and with a cry
Fled to the icy north, the timid Spring
Arose in snowdrops, and the days grew long.
Spring touched the black pots on my window-sill,
And, though begrimed and foul with dust and soot,
The blind plants felt it in their withered veins,
And smiled a sickly green. One Sabbath day,
I left my mother's dwelling in the morn

Behind; the pleading and the scolding bells
Disturbed the peaceful air. " 'T is ever so—
Religion's pure serene is vexed and torn
By raging sectaries. In every street
The brave streams of the proud and gaudy world
Flow to the house of God.—My mother sits
With vanished shapes, and faces of the dead,
And little pattering footsteps: why should she,
A broken heart wrapt up in faded silk,
Mix with the prosperous? 'T is very well;
Let the white faces creep into their graves,
And leave pomp in the sun." The shining day
Spread out before me, and I wandered on
Free as those vagrant children of the waste,
Shadow and sunshine. By the sandy banks
Of a shrunk stream, that in unnumbered rills
Tinkled 'tween pebbles and hot glistening stones,
Two green kingfishers played. A travelling shower
O'ertook me on my way; I stood and heard
The skylarks singing in the sunny rain,

With a dim recognition in my heart
As if I knew the meaning of the song
In some forgotten life. I reached a height
Which lay from fairy fern to stately tree
Asleep in sunshine. From its crown I saw
The country fade into the distant sky,
With happy hamlets drowned in apple-bloom,
And ivy-muffled churches still with graves,
And restless fires subdued and tamed by day,
And scattered towns whence came at intervals
Upon the wind, a sweet clear sound of bells;
Through all, a river, like a stream of haze,
Drew its slow length until 'twas lost in woods.
Still as a lichened stone I lay and watched
The lights and shadows on the landscape's face,
The moving cloud that quenched the shining fields,
The gliding sunbeam, the grey trailing shower,
And all the commerce of the earth and sky.
With weary limbs at sunset I returned;
And in the dingy fringes of the town,

The helpless languor of the Sabbath-eve,
The listless groups that stood around the doors,
The silent children, and the smoke that rose
Lazy and spiritless into the air,
Told the world's sinews had been overwrought
And now hung lax and loose. My spirits fell,
Sheer as a skylark when his song is o'er;
I crept into my little twilight room,
And there my day of glory set in tears.

Next morn the bells awoke me to my toil,
And what a pageant of divinest sights
Passed by me on my daily round of life!
I bore a message, and upon my way
The streets were swept by the impetuous rain,
The lightning fluttered in my dazzled eyes,
And thunder like a sea broke overhead.
A fleece of thunder hung before the sun
With a wild blazing fringe, while scattered shreds
Burned on the marble sky. Black strings of ships

Sat on the angry mirror of the stream
Keen with the splendour, till the gusty rain
Drowned the red sunset and the winds were loud.

For years and years continually were mine
The long dull roar of traffic, and at night
The mighty pathos of the empty streets.
I leant at midnight o'er the lonely bridge,
And heard the water slipping 'neath the arch :
" Man flies from solitude and dwells in noise,
Like one who has a pale wronged face at home
On which he dares not look ; to calm his heart
The world must roar with traffic, brawl with war.
What need to strive for wealth, opinion, praise,
Wherewith to drug our spirits and forget ?
Thou bearest in thy heart, black glittering stream,
A deeper rest for the unfortunate
Than Pluto's gold can buy. Ah ! Pleasure, Fame,
But crown pale mortals with an envied pain ;
Death pities, and gives sleep. A thousand years

This river wandered through an empty waste
Where no man's voice was heard, and mournful winds
Shook sighing sedges as they swept along,
And blurred the silver of the lonely moon.
Huts rose upon its banks, then sank in flame,
And rose from ashes. Slow the city grew,
Like coral reef on which the builders die
Until it stands complete in pain and death.
Great bridges with their coronets of lamps
Light the black stream beneath ; rude ocean's flock,
Ships from all climes, are folded in its docks ;
And every heart from its great central dome
To farthest suburb is a darkened stage
On which Grief walks alone. A thousand years !
The idle Summer will amuse herself
Dressing the front where merchants congregate,
And where the mighty war-horse snorts in bronze,
With clasping flowers ; where now the evening street
Rolls gay with life,—in silence and the dew
The hamadryad issues from the tree,

Like music from an instrument." How strange
When the chill morn was breaking in the east
Looked the familiar streets! In pallid squares
I stood awe-struck, like a bewildered soul
In the great dawn of death. Each house was blind,
Closed 'gainst the light, and slow it filled the street,
Unsoiled by smoke, unscared by any sound;
It entered trembling rude and haggard lanes
Where riot but an hour before had brawled
Himself to rest. St. Stephen's golden vane
Burned in the early beam, which glimmered down,
Making the old spire gay. The swallows woke,
And jerked and twittered in the shining air;
Broad Labour turned and muttered in his sleep;
And the first morning cart began to roll.

I saw a son weep o'er a mother's grave:
"Ay, weep, poor boy—weep thy most bitter tears
That thou shalt smile so soon. We bury Love,
Forgetfulness grows over it like grass;

That is a thing to weep for, not the dead."
The weeks flew on and beautified my grief:
I stood within a torrent's drenching spray,
Up rose the sun, with happy eyes I saw
The sounding chasm struck with precious light,
The boiling wreaths transformed to sunny mist
On which an iris played. A little child
Watching the fringe of radiance o'er the hill,
Stops on its way and with suspended breath
Awaits the golden moon;—so did my life
Await some unknown joy. A haunting face
Disturbed me with its beauty, and at night
It looked upon me through the roof of dreams;
My heart like a touched harp-string thrilled, and bliss
Crept through my veins like that which stirs a tree
From knotted root up to its slenderest spray
Touched by the hand of Spring. One night alone
I sat beside the dull and covered fire,
And gave myself up to the phantom joy:
Methought I heard a sound, methought it came

From my poor mother's room; I softly crept,
And listened; in the middle of the night
I heard her talk with God.—"Thou knowest well
That Sorrow has been with me like a babe
In my great solitude, till I have come
To love its smileless face. Thou, Love, who wrapt
Thyself in flesh, and sat awhile disguised
At the rude feast of our Humanity,
And tasted every sweet and bitter there,
Then rose and unsuspected went away;
Who loved the humble ones at Bethany;
Who wept o'er Lazarus, and with thy tears
Comforted all the family of grief
In every time, in every far off land;—
Thou, infinite Tenderness, wilt pardon me
If my heart murmured when my lips were still.
Our life is noble, Thou hast breathed its air;
Death sweet, for Thou hast died. On Thy way home
One night thou slept'st within the dreadful grave,
And took away its fear. Oh, smile on me!

The world and I have done: with humble heart
I sit down at thy glorious gates and wait
Till death shall lead me in. But chiefly bless
My poor boy left alone in this ill world:
I never more may look upon his face,
May never hear his voice. Thou know'st him well,
For every morning, long before the lark
Sang at Thy shining doors, my prayer arose
To crave Thy blessing on his restless youth.
It is the evening of my day of life,
I have been working from the early dawn,
Am sore and weary; let me go to sleep,—
Let me stretch out my limbs and be at rest
In the untroubled silence of the grave."
My heart swelled like a man's, who after years
Wasted in riot 'neath a tropic sky,
Returns, and wandering on a Sabbath-eve
Bursts into tears beside a twilight church,
Filled with a psalm which he knew long ago
When his heart too was pure.

When thunder blots the sun,
And lays a hand of terror on the herds,
That stills the bleating on a hundred hills,
There is a silence over all the land
Waiting the fluttering fire. So did I wait,
And swift as lightning fell the blow on me.
Reason had left her throne, and busy dreams
Made a wild medley of the day,—as when
Some great event has happened in the tower,
After the lord and lady have retired
The rude domestics give it strangest shapes,
Talking around the fire—and suddenly,
With an affrighted heart I lay awake,
And listened eager as alarmed air
Which has been traversed by a sudden cry.
A moment told me all; I ran to her,
But she had sunk in swoon, and there I stood
Like one too late upon a brink, who sees
The water closing over all he loves.
I knelt down by the bed. "Come, Margery!

The sea is glittering in the sunny bay,
The fisher's nets are drying on the shore,
And let us gather silver purple shells
For necklaces. You have been in the woods;
Your lips are black with berries. O the boats,
The bonny, bonny boats! List, the fishers sing!"

"O, mother, mother!"
"They have left me here,
Upon this dark and dreadful, dreadful road;
I cannot hear a voice or touch a hand;
O Father, take me home!" She sobbed and wept
As if she were a little wandered child.
Her Father took her home. I stooped to catch
Her feeble breath; a change came o'er her look,
A flutter in her throat, and all was peace.
Then slowly I grew conscious that the dawn
Filled the square window with his hateful face,
Staring into the chamber of the dead,—
And with affrighted eyes I gazed on him.

THE CHANGE.

THE CHANGE.

"Oh! never, never can I call
Another morning to my day,
And now through shade to shade I fall
From afternoon to evening grey."
In bitterness these words I said,
And lo! when I expected least,—
For day was gone,—a moonrise spread
Its emerald radiance up the east.

By passion's gaudy candle-lights,
I sat and watched the world's brave play;
Blown out,—how poor the trains and sights
Looked in the cruel light of day!

I cursed Man for his spaniel heart,
His bounded brain, his lust of pelf—
Alas! each crime of field and mart
Lived in a dark disease of self.

I saw the smiles and mean salaams
Of slavish hearts; I heard the cry
Of maddened people's throwing palms
Before each cheered and timbreled lie.
I loathed the brazen front and brag
Of bloated time; in self-defence
Withdrew I to my lonely crag,
And fortress of indifference.

But Nature is revenged on those
Who turn from her to lonely days:
Contentment, like the speedwell, blows
Along the common-beaten ways.
The dead and thick green-mantled moats
That gird my house resembled me,

Or some long-weeded hull that rots
Upon a glazing tropic sea.

And madness ever round us lies,
The final bourne and end of thought;
And Pleasure shuts her glorious eyes
At one cold glance and melts to nought;
And Nature cannot hear us moan;
She smiles in sunshine, raves in rain—
The music breathed by Love alone
Can ease the world's immortal pain.

The sun for ever hastes sublime,
Waved onward by Orion's lance;
Obedient to the spheral chime,
Across the world the seasons dance;
The flaming elements ne'er bewail
Their iron bounds, their less or more;
The sea can drown a thousand sail,
Yet rounds the pebbles on the shore.

I looked with pride on what I'd done,
I counted merits o'er anew,
In presence of the burning sun,
Which drinks me like a drop of dew.
A lofty scorn I dared to shed
On human passions, hopes, and jars,
I—standing on the countless dead,
And pitied by the countless stars.

But mine is now a humbled heart,
My lonely pride is weak as tears;
No more I seek to stand apart,
A mocker of the rolling years.
Imprisoned in this wintry clime,
I've found enough, O Lord of breath,
Enough to plume the feet of time,
Enough to hide the eyes of death.

R. CLAY, PRINTER, BREAD STREET HILL.

BY THE REV. CHARLES KINGSLEY,

RECTOR OF EVERSLEY, AND CANON OF MIDDLEHAM.
AUTHOR OF "WESTWARD HO!" &c. &c.

A Third Edition of

GLAUCUS;

OR, THE WONDERS OF THE SHORE.

With a Frontispiece. Fcap. 8vo. beautifully bound in cloth, with gilt leaves, 3*s*. 6*d*.

OPINIONS.

GUARDIAN.

"As useful and exciting a sea-side companion as we have ever seen."

ECLECTIC REVIEW.

"Its pages sparkle with life, they open up a thousand sources of unanticipated pleasure, and combine amusement with instruction in a very happy and unwonted degree."

SPECTATOR.

"The general remarks show wide sympathy, deep thought, and rich eloquence."

EXAMINER.

"We cannot be too grateful to Mr. Kingsley for his 'Glaucus.'"

EDINBURGH GUARDIAN.

"Its inward and outward beauty will assuredly attract and rivet many a reader."

CHRISTIAN REMEMBRANCER.

"A pleasant and cheerful sea-side book."

COMMONWEALTH.

"The style is vivid and expressive; the spirit good; the matter fascinating and substantial."

ANNALS OF NATURAL HISTORY.

"One of the most charming works on Natural History . . . . written in such a style and adorned with such a variety of illustration, that we question whether the most unconcerned reader can peruse it without deriving both pleasure and profit."

BIBLIOTHECA SACRA (American).

"A most interesting little work."

BY GEORGE WILSON, M.D., F.R.S.E.

REGIUS PROFESSOR OF TECHNOLOGY IN THE UNIVERSITY OF EDINBURGH; PRESIDENT OF THE ROYAL SCOTTISH SOCIETY OF ARTS; AND DIRECTOR OF THE INDUSTRIAL MUSEUM OF SCOTLAND.

THE

FIVE GATEWAYS OF KNOWLEDGE.

In fcap. 8vo. cloth, 2*s.* 6*d.*

OPINIONS.

SPECTATOR.

"At once attractive and useful. . . . The manner is vivacious and clear; the matter is closely packed, but without confusion."

JOHN BULL.

"Charms and enlivens the attention whilst the heart and understanding are improved. . . It is an invaluable little book."

NONCONFORMIST.

"This is a beautifully written and altogether delightful little book on the five senses."

CRITIC.

"As a means to teach the great truth that we are 'fearfully and wonderfully made,' this essay will be of great value."

EXAMINER.

"An extremely pleasant little book . . . . entertaining and instructive; and may be welcomed in many a home."

LEADER.

"Dr. Wilson unites poetic with scientific faculty, and this union gives a charm to all he writes. In the little volume before us he has described the five senses in language so popular that a child may comprehend the meaning, so suggestive that philosophers will read it with pleasure."

LITERARY SPECTATOR.

"Besides the merit of being deeply interesting, it can also lay claim to the higher functions of a useful instructor; and in its twofold capacity it has our unqualified approval."

SCOTTISH PRESS.

"Every page presents us with something worthy of being thought about; every one is bright with the full clear light of the writer's mind, and with his genial humour."

Cambridge, April, 1857.

A LIST OF

New Books and New Editions,

PUBLISHED BY MACMILLAN & Co.

BY ALEXANDER SMITH,

Secretary to the University of Edinburgh, and Author of "A Life Drama and other Poems."

A New Volume of Poems. Fcap. 8vo. cloth. *In the Press.*

BY GEORGE WILSON, M.D., F.R.S.E.

Regius Professor of Technology in the University of Edinburgh; President of the Royal Scottish Society of Arts; and Director of the Industrial Museum of Scotland.

The Five Gateways of Knowledge.

In fcap. 8vo. cloth, 2*s*. 6*d*.; or elegantly bound in cloth, with richly gilt back and sides, and with gilt leaves, suitable for Prizes or Presents, price 3*s*. 6*d*.

OPINIONS OF THE PRESS.

"*At once attractive and useful. . . . The manner is vivacious and clear; the matter is closely packed, but without confusion.*"—SPECTATOR, Nov. 8, 1856.

"*An extremely pleasant little book . . . entertaining and instructive; and may be welcomed in many a home.*"—THE EXAMINER, Nov. 15, 1856.

"*Dr. Wilson unites poetic with scientific faculty, and this union gives a charm to all he writes. In the little volume before us he has described the five senses in language so popular that a child may comprehend the meaning, so suggestive that philosophers will read it with pleasure.*"—THE LEADER, Nov. 22, 1856.

"*Every page presents us with something worthy of being thought about; every one is bright with the full clear light of the writer's mind, and with his genial humour.*"—THE SCOTTISH PRESS, Nov. 21, 1856.

A NEW NOVEL.

BY AN OLD BOY.

Tom Brown's School-Days.

In crown 8vo. cloth, 10*s*. 6*d*. *Just published.*

THE WORKS OF

THE REV. WILLIAM ARCHER BUTLER,

Late Professor of Moral Philosophy in the University of Dublin.

Uniformly printed and bound, 5 vols. 8vo. cloth, £2 18*s.*

" *A man of glowing genius and diversified accomplishments, whose remains fill these five brilliant volumes.*"—EDINBURGH REVIEW, July, 1856.

" *One destined, if we mistake not, to take the highest place among writers of our English tongue.*"—NORTH BRITISH REVIEW, Feb. 1856.

" *Poet, orator, metaphysician, theologian, 'nihil tetigit quod non ornavit.'* "
DUBLIN UNIVERSITY MAGAZINE.

" *Discrimination and earnestness, beauty and power, a truly philosophical spirit.*"
BRITISH QUARTERLY.

" *A burning and a shining light.*"—BISHOP OF EXETER.

" *Entitled to stand in the front rank, not merely of ministers of the Irish Church, but of the wisest and best teachers of all denominations.*"
WESLEYAN MAGAZINE, Feb. 1856.

ALSO SOLD SEPARATELY AS FOLLOWS.

1. *A Fourth Edition of* Sermons Doctrinal and Practical. FIRST SERIES. Edited by the Very Rev. T. WOODWARD, M.A. Dean of Down, with a Memoir and Portrait. 8vo. cloth, 12*s.*

" *Present a richer combination of the qualities for Sermons of the first class than any we have met with in any living writer.*"—BRITISH QUARTERLY.

2. *A Second Edition of a Second Series of* Sermons, Doctrinal and Practical. Edited from the Author's MSS., by J. A. JEREMIE, D.D., Regius Professor of Divinity in the University of Cambridge. 8vo. cloth, 10*s.* 6*d.*

" *They are marked by the same originality and vigour of expression, the same richness of imagery and illustration, the same large views and catholic spirit, and the same depth and fervour of devotional feeling, which so remarkably distinguished the preceding Series and which rendered it a most valuable accession to our theological literature.*"—From DR. JEREMIE'S PREFACE.

" *Distinguished by the point and vigour of their style, the happiness of their illustrations, and the largeness of their views.*"—ATHENÆUM, Feb. 9, 1856.

" *All exceedingly beautiful and valuable.*"—LITERARY CHURCHMAN.

REV. ARCHER BUTLER'S WORKS.

3. **Letters on Romanism.** A Reply to DR. NEWMAN'S Essay on Development. Edited by the Very Rev. T. WOODWARD, M.A. Dean of Down. 8vo. cloth, 10*s*. 6*d*.

"*A work which ought to be in the Library of every Student of Divinity.*"
BISHOP OF ST. DAVID'S.

"*There are books which while elicited by temporary controversy become so rich in genius as to possess a permanent value. The book before us is of that rare class.*"—BRITISH QUARTERLY, Jan. 1855.

"*One of the ablest refutations of Romanism in its latest and most refined form.*" —NORTH BRITISH REVIEW, Feb. 1856.

"*Deserve to be considered the most remarkable proofs of the Author's indomitable energy and power of concentration.*"—EDINBURGH REVIEW, July, 1856.

4. **Lectures on the History of Ancient Philosophy.** Edited from the Author's MSS., with Notes, by WILLIAM HEPWORTH THOMPSON, M.A., Regius Professor of Greek in the University of Cambridge. 2 vols. 8vo., £1 5*s*.

"*I have seen enough of them to be convinced of their great scientific value; and am much gratified in finding so important a subject treated with so much learning and acuteness.*"—SIR WM. HAMILTON, Professor of Logic and Metaphysics, Edinburgh, Feb. 27, 1856.

"*Many a good Greek scholar must have lived and died with less of a real knowledge of Plato after years of study, than a thoughtful English reader may receive from this book in a week.*"—EXAMINER, April, 1856.

"*No man in England is more competent than Professor Thompson to pronounce upon the value of any contribution to this branch of ancient learning; and he says,—*

"'*Of the dialectic and physics of Plato they are the only exposition at once full, accurate, and popular, with which I am acquainted: being far more accurate than the French, and incomparably more popular than the German treatises on these departments of the Platonic philosophy.*'

"*We must not dismiss Professor Butler's Lectures without testifying to the admirable editing to which they have been submitted.*"
SPECTATOR, May 3, 1856.

"*We are confident that every intelligent reader will join in the high encomium which the learned Editor has pronounced upon them.*"
EDINBURGH REVIEW, July, 1856.

LECTURES TO LADIES ON PRACTICAL SUBJECTS.

Third Edition, revised. Crown 8vo. cloth, *7s. 6d.*

CONTENTS:—INTRODUCTORY LECTURE. Plan of a Female College for the Help of the Rich and the Poor.—I. The College and the Hospital. By the Rev. F. D. MAURICE—II. The Country Parish. By the Rev. C. KINGSLEY—III. On Over-work, Distress, and Anxiety, as Causes of Mental and Bodily Disease. By GEORGE JOHNSON, M.D., Fellow of the Royal College of Physicians, Physician to King's College Hospital—IV. On Dispensaries and Allied Institutions. By EDWARD H. SIEVEKING, M.D., Fellow of the Royal College of Physicians—V. District Visiting. By the Rev. J. LL. DAVIES, Fellow of Trinity College, Cambridge, and Rector of Christ Church, Marylebone—VI. The Influence of Occupation on Health. By Dr. CHAMBERS, Physician to St. Mary's Hospital—VII. On Law as it affects the Poor. By FITZJAMES STEPHEN, LL.B. of the Inner Temple, Barrister-at-Law—VIII. On the Every-day Work of Ladies. By ARCHDEACON ALLEN—IX. On Teaching by Words. By the Very Rev. DEAN TRENCH—X. On Sanitary Law. By TOM TAYLOR, Esq., Secretary to the General Board of Health—XI. Workhouse Visiting. By the Rev. J. S. BREWER—POSTSCRIPT.

"*A glance at the subjects treated of, and a bare enumeration of the names of the gentlemen who delivered the lectures, should be enough to ensure careful attention to them. . . . . These men, themselves an honour to their times, do honour to woman by giving her the benefit of the best thoughts of manly minds.*"—EDINBURGH REVIEW, *Jan.* 1856.

"*We scarcely know a volume containing more sterling good sense, or a finer expression of modern intelligence on social subjects.*'—CHAMBERS' JOURNAL, Nov. 22, 1856.

BY THE LATE HENRY LUSHINGTON, AND FRANKLIN LUSHINGTON.

La Nation Boutiquière: and other Poems, chiefly Political. With a Preface. By HENRY LUSHINGTON.
POINTS OF WAR. By FRANKLIN LUSHINGTON.

In 1 vol. fcap. 8vo. cloth, 3*s.*

"*Full of truth and warmth, and noble life.........In these few pages are contained some of the last thoughts of a fine-hearted man of genius.........One of a class that must be ranked among the rarest of our time.*"—EXAMINER Aug. 18, 1855.

BY JULIUS CHARLES HARE, M.A.,

Late Archdeacon of Lewes, and Rector of Herstmonceux, Chaplain in Ordinary to the Queen, and formerly Fellow of Trinity College, Cambridge.

UNIFORMLY PRINTED AND BOUND IN CLOTH.

1. Charges to the Clergy of the Archdeaconry of Lewes. Delivered at the Ordinary Visitations from the year 1840 to 1854, with Notes on the Principal Events affecting the Church during that period. With an Introduction, explanatory of his position in the Church, with reference to the Parties which divide it. 3 vols. 8vo. cloth, £1 11*s*. 6*d*.

2. Charges to the Clergy of the Archdeaconry of Lewes. Delivered at the Ordinary Visitations in the years 1843, 1845, 1846. Never before published. With an Introduction, explanatory of his position in the Church, with reference to the Parties that divide it. 8vo. cloth, 6*s*. 6*d*.

   This is included in the 3 vols. of collected Charges, but is published separately for the sake of those who have the rest.

3. Miscellaneous Pamphlets on some of the Leading Questions agitated in the Church during the last Ten Years. 8vo. cloth, 12*s*.

4. *A Second Edition of* Vindication of Luther against his recent English Assailants. 8vo. cloth, 7*s*.

5. *A Second Edition of* The Mission of the Comforter. With Notes. 8vo. cloth, 12*s*.

6. *A Second Series of* Parish Sermons. 8vo. cloth, 12*s*.

7. *A Second Edition of* The Victory of Faith. 8vo. cloth, 5*s*.

8. *A Second Edition of* The Contest with Rome. A Charge, delivered in 1851. With Notes, especially in answer to Dr. Newman's recent Lectures. 8vo. cloth, 10*s*. 6*d*.

   This is included in the 3 vols. of Charges.

BY JOHN McLEOD CAMPBELL.

The Nature of the Atonement, and its Relation to Remission of Sins and Eternal Life. 8vo. cloth, 10*s*. 6*d*.

"*This is a remarkable book, as indicating the mode in which a devout and intellectual mind has found its way, almost unassisted, out of the extreme Lutheran and Calvinistic views of the Atonement into a healthier atmosphere of doctrine. . . . We cannot assent to all the positions laid down by this writer, but he is entitled to be spoken respectfully of, both because of his evident earnestness and reality, and the tender mode in which he deals with the opinions of others from whom he feels compelled to differ.*"—LITERARY CHURCHMAN, March 8, 1856.

"*Deserves wide celebrity.*"—CHRISTIAN TIMES.

BY THE REV. G. E. LYNCH COTTON, M.A.,

Master of Marlborough College, Examining Chaplain to the Bishop of London, formerly Fellow of Trinity College, Cambridge.

Sermons: Chiefly connected with Public Events, 1854.
Fcap. 8vo. cloth, 3*s*.

"*A volume of which we can speak with high admiration.*"
CHRISTIAN REMEMBRANCER.

BY THE RIGHT REV. JOHN WILLIAM COLENSO, D.D.,

Lord Bishop of Natal, formerly Fellow of St. John's College, Cambridge.

1. **Ten Weeks in Natal.** A Journal of a First Tour of Visitation among the Colonists and Zulu Kaffirs of Natal. With four Lithographs and a Map. Fcap. 8vo. cloth, 5*s*.

"*A most interesting and charmingly written little book.*"—EXAMINER.

"*The Church has good reason to be grateful for the publication.*"
COLONIAL CHURCH CHRONICLE.

2. *A Second Edition of* **Village Sermons.**
Fcap. 8vo. cloth, 2*s*. 6*d*.

3. **Companion to the Communion.** The Communion Service from the Prayer Book: with Select Readings from the Writings of the Rev. F. D. MAURICE. Fine Edition, rubricated and bound in morocco antique, gilt edges, 6*s*.; or in cloth, red edges, 2*s*. 6*d*.; common paper, limp cloth, 1*s*.

BY THE AUTHOR OF "VISITING MY RELATIONS."

Waters of Comfort. A small Volume of Devotional Poetry of a Practical Character. Fcap. 8vo. cloth, 4*s*. *Just ready.*

Depth of thought, closeness and force of expression......call to mind the sacred poets of the 17th century."—SPECTATOR.

"*A very beautiful little volume of verse it is,—meditative, spiritual, and practical.*"—NONCONFORMIST.

BY THE REV. CHARLES KINGSLEY, F.S.A.

Rector of Eversley, and Canon of Middleham.

1. *A Second Edition of* Two Years Ago.
3 vols. crown 8vo. cloth, £1 11*s.* 6*d.* *Just ready.*

"*Much the best book Mr. Kingsley has written.*"—SATURDAY REVIEW.

2. The Heroes: Greek Fairy Tales for my Children.
With Eight Illustrations drawn on wood by the Author. Beautifully printed on tinted paper and elegantly bound in cloth, with gilt leaves, 7*s.* 6*d.*

"*The fascination of a fairy tale is given to each legend.*"—EXAMINER.

"MR. KINGSLEY *has imbued his narrative with a classical feeling, and thrown over it the glow of a rich imagination and a poetical spirit.*"—SPECTATOR.

"*It is admirably adapted for the perusal of young people, who will grow both wiser and merrier while they read.*"—MORNING POST, Jan. 4, 1856.

"*If the public accepts our recommendation, this book will run through many editions.*"—GUARDIAN, March 12, 1856.

3. *A Second Edition of* "Westward Ho!" or the Voyages and Adventures of Sir Amyas Leigh, Knight, of Borrough, in the County of Devon, in the reign of Her most Glorious Majesty Queen Elizabeth. Rendered into modern English. 3 vols. crown 8vo. cloth, £1 11*s.* 6*d.*

"MR. KINGSLEY *has selected a good subject, and has written a good novel to excellent purpose.*"—THE TIMES, Aug. 18, 1855.

"*Noble and well-timed.*"—SPECTATOR.

4. *A Third Edition of* Glaucus; or, the Wonders of the Shore. With a Frontispiece. Fcap. 8vo. beautifully bound in cloth, with gilt leaves, 3*s.* 6*d.*

"*As useful and exciting a sea-side companion as we have ever seen.*"—GUARDIAN.

"*Its pages sparkle with life, they open up a thousand sources of unanticipated pleasure, and combine amusement with instruction in a very happy and unwonted degree.*"—ECLECTIC REVIEW.

5. *A Second Edition of* Phaethon; or, Loose Thoughts for Loose Thinkers. Crown 8vo. boards, 2*s.*

"*Its suggestions may meet half way many a latent doubt, and, like a light breeze, lift from the soul clouds that are gathering heavily, and threatening to settle down in wintry gloom on the summer of many a fair and promising young life.*" —SPECTATOR.

"*One of the most interesting works we ever read.*"—NONCONFORMIST.

6. Alexandria and Her Schools. Being Four Lectures delivered at the Philosophical Institution, Edinburgh. With a Preface. Crown 8vo. cloth, 5*s.*

"*A series of brilliant biographical and literary sketches, interspersed with comments of the closest modern, or rather universal application.*"—SPECTATOR.

LORD ARTHUR HERVEY, M.A.

Rector of Ickworth-with-Horinger.

1. The Genealogies of our Lord and Saviour Jesus Christ, as contained in the Gospels of St. Matthew and St. Luke, reconciled with each other and with the Genealogy of the House of David, from Adam to the close of the Canon of the Old Testament, and shown to be in harmony with the true Chronology of the Times. 8vo. cloth, 10*s.* 6*d.*

"*The production of a thorough scholar.*"—BRITISH QUARTERLY.

"*An addition of mark to our Library of Biblical Criticism.*"—GUARDIAN.

"*It seems to us that in view of the kind of criticism to which the Old and New Testament records are now subjected, his work has special importance and claims.*"—NONCONFORMIST.

"*We commend* LORD HERVEY'S *book to our readers as a valuable storehouse of information on this important subject, and as indicative of an approximation towards a solution of the difficulties with which it is beset.*"—JOURNAL OF SACRED LITERATURE.

2. The Inspiration of Holy Scripture. Five Sermons Preached before the University in the month of December, 1855. 8vo. cloth, 3*s.* 6*d.*

"*A valuable addition to his former excellent work.*"
BRITISH BANNER, March 13, 1856.

"*Seasonable and valuable.*"—BRITISH AND FOREIGN EVANGELICAL REVIEW.

"*Give good proof that the writer is himself a careful student of the sacred volume.*"—LITERARY CHURCHMAN, May 3, 1856.

BY THE RIGHT REV. CHARLES PERRY, D.D.,

Lord Bishop of Melbourne, formerly Fellow and Tutor of Trinity College, Cambridge.

Five Sermons, Preached before the University of Cambridge in the month of November, 1855.
Crown 8vo. cloth, 3*s.* *Just ready.*

"*These Sermons exhibit a serious earnestness, and the results of scholarly training, showing themselves in a clear and forcible style.*"—SPECTATOR, March 8, 1856.

"*Catholic in spirit, and evangelical in sentiment.*"
EVANGELICAL MAGAZINE, May, 1856.

BY ISAAC TAYLOR, ESQ.,

Author of "The Natural History of Enthusiasm."

The Restoration of Belief.
Crown 8vo. cloth, 8*s.* 6*d.*

"*A volume which contains logical sagacity, and philosophic comprehension, as well as the magnanimity and courage of faith, in richer profusion than any other work bearing on religious matters that has been addressed to this generation. 'The Restoration of Belief' may, in many respects, take a place among the books of the nineteenth century, corresponding to that justly conceded by us to the 'Analogy' of Butler in the literature of the last age, or to the 'Thoughts' of Pascal in that of the age preceding.*"
NORTH BRITISH REVIEW, Nov. 1855.

"*A book which I would recommend to every student.*"—REV. C. A. SWAINSON, Principal of Chichester Theological College.

BY GEORGE BOOLE, LL.D.,

Professor of Mathematics in Queen's College, Cork.

The Philosophy of Logic.

8vo. cloth. *Nearly ready.*

BY BROOKE FOSS WESTCOTT, M.A.

Late Fellow of Trinity College, and

FENTON JOHN ANTHONY HORT, M.A.

Fellow of Trinity College.

The New Testament in the Original Greek:

The Text Revised. *Preparing.*

BY CHARLES COLLIER, M.D. F.R.S.,

Fellow of the Royal College of Physicians.

Aristotle on the Vital Principle.

Translated from the Original Text, with Notes. Crown 8vo. cloth, 8*s.* 6*d.*

"*Has rendered the original into elegant and idiomatic English..........An important feature of the work lies in the notes, in which the learned translator comments on Aristotle's physiological facts and conclusions, illustrating or amending them by the results of modern science. The utility of the translation is further enhanced by the addition of preludes to each chapter, in which the scope of the argument is briefly stated.*"—BRITISH QUARTERLY, Jan., 1856.

BY THE RIGHT REV. GEORGE AUGUSTUS SELWYN, D.D.,

Lord Bishop of New Zealand, formerly Fellow of St. John's College, Cambridge.

A Third Edition of The Work of Christ in the World.

Four Sermons, Preached before the University of Cambridge on the Four Sundays preceding Advent, in the Year of our Lord, 1854. Published for the benefit of the New Zealand Church Fund. Crown 8vo. 2*s.*

BY J. LLEWELLYN DAVIES, M.A.

Fellow of Trinity College, and Rector of Christ Church, Marylebone.

St. Paul and Modern Thought: Remarks on some

of the Views advanced in PROFESSOR JOWETT'S Commentary on St. Paul. 8vo. sewed, 2*s.* 6*d.*

"*We can heartily recommend Mr. Davies's Essay.*"—SPECTATOR, April 26, 1856.

"*A piece of profound as well as genial criticism.*"—NATIONAL REVIEW.

"*Especially remarkable for philosophical depth and power of argument.*"—CHRISTIAN REMEMBRANCER.

BY REV. D. J. VAUGHAN, M.A.

Fellow of Trinity College, Cambridge, and Incumbent of St. Mark's, Whitechapel, London.

Sermons Preached in St. John's Church, Leicester,

during the Years 1855 and 1856. Crown 8vo. cloth, 5*s*. 6*d*.

Just ready.

BY MACVEY NAPIER, ESQ.,

Late Editor of the "Edinburgh Review," and of the "Encyclopædia Britannica."

Lord Bacon and Sir Walter Raleigh.

Critical and Biographical Essays. Post 8vo. cloth, 7*s*. 6*d*.

"*The Article on Bacon is clear, accurate, convincing, complete. The Article on Raleigh is very valuable, first, because* MR. NAPIER *has had access to many documents unknown to former biographers, and next, because he completely clears Raleigh from the old imputation of deceit about the Guiana mine, as well as of the other minor charges.*"—NORTH BRITISH REVIEW.

BY J. E. B. MAYOR, M.A.,

Fellow and Assistant Tutor of St. John's College.

1. Lives of Nicholas Ferrar, of Clare Hall.

By his Brother John, and Dr. Jebb. Now first edited, with Illustrations. Fcap. 8vo. 7*s*. 6*d*.

2. Autobiography of Matthew Robinson.

Now first Edited. With Illustrations. Fcap. 8vo. cloth, 5*s*. 6*d*.

Just ready.

BY JOSEPH FRANCIS THRUPP, M.A.,

Vicar of Barrington, Cambridgeshire, late Fellow of Trinity College.

Antient Jerusalem.

A New Investigation into the History, Topography, and Plan of the City, Environs, and Temple. Designed principally to illustrate the records and prophecies of Scripture. With Map and Plans. 8vo. cloth, 15*s*.

"*He is calm and candid, and has a thorough acquaintance with all that has been written upon his subject.*"—ATHENÆUM.

"*A book of no ordinary value. Patient research, candour, and a reverence for divine truth distinguish the whole volume.*"—JOURNAL OF SACRED LITERATURE.

"*A well-directed and able endeavour to throw additional light upon the history and topography of the Holy City. Those who read it will find reason to be grateful to the author.*"—LITERARY CHURCHMAN.

BY X and Y (Two Unknown Quantities).

A Long Vacation Ramble in Norway and Sweden.

"*Skaal to the Northland, Skaal!*"

"*And dark, and true, and tender is the North.*"

In crown 8vo. cloth, 6*s*. 6*d*. *Just ready.*

BY THOMAS RAWSON BIRKS, M.A.,

RECTOR OF KELSHALL, FORMERLY FELLOW OF TRINITY COLLEGE,

Author of "The Life of the Rev. E. Bickersteth."

The Difficulties of Belief, in connexion with the Creation and the Fall.

Crown 8vo. cloth, 4*s*. 6*d*.

"*Without binding ourselves to the immediate acceptance of this interesting volume, we may yet express our hearty approbation of its tone.*"
CHRISTIAN REMEMBRANCER, April, 1856.

"*A profound and masterly essay.*"—ECLECTIC, May, 1856.

"*His arguments are original, and carefully and logically elaborated. We may add that they are distinguished by a marked sobriety and reverence for the Word of God.*"—RECORD.

"*Of sterling value.*"—LONDON QUARTERLY.

BY THE HON. HENRY E. J. HOWARD, D.D.,

Dean of Lichfield.

1. **The Book of Genesis, according to the Version of the LXX.** Translated into English, with Notices of its Omissions and Insertions, and with Notes on the Passages in which it differs from our Authorized Version. Crown 8vo. cloth, 8*s*. 6*d*.

"*The Work deserves high commendation; it is an excellent introduction to the comparative study of God's Word, in these three languages with which an ordinary English student is mainly, if not entirely concerned.*"—GUARDIAN.

2. **The Books of Exodus and Leviticus.** Crown 8vo. uniform with the above, cloth, 10*s*. 6*d*.

BY THE REV. C. A. SWAINSON, M.A.

Principal of the Chichester Theological College.

A Handbook to Butler's Analogy; with a few Notes.

Crown 8vo. sewed, 1*s*. 6*d*.

BY CHARLES HARDWICK, M.A.

Christian Advocate in the University of Cambridge.

Christ and other Masters: An Historical Inquiry into some of the chief Parallelisms and Contrasts between Christianity and the Religious Systems of the Ancient World; with special reference to prevailing Difficulties and Objections. Part I. Introduction. Part II. Religions of India.

In 8vo. cloth, 7*s*. 6*d*. each.

BY CHARLES MANSFIELD, M.A.

1. **Letters from Paraguay, Brazil, and the Plate.** By the late CHARLES MANSFIELD, M.A., Clare Hall, Cambridge. With a life by CHARLES KINGSLEY, Rector of Eversley. Post 8vo. With a Map, and a Portrait, and numerous Woodcuts. 12*s*. 6*d*.

Just ready.

"*An interesting and instructive volume.*"—MORNING POST.

"*A delightfully written book.*"—BRITISH QUARTERLY.

"*Full of varied matter and earnest thought.*"—NEW QUARTERLY.

2. **On the Constitution of Salts.** Edited from the Author's MS. by N. H. S. MASKELYNE, M.A., Wadham College, and Reader in Mineralogy in the University of Oxford. *In the Press.*

BY C. MANSFIELD INGLEBY, M.A.

Of Trinity College, Cambridge;
Teacher of Logic in the Industrial Department of the Birmingham and Midland Institute.

Outlines of Theoretical Logic. Founded on the New Analytic of SIR WILLIAM HAMILTON. Designed for a Text-book in Schools and Colleges.

In Fcap. 8vo. cloth, 3*s*. 6*d*. *Just ready.*

BY THE LATE HENRY MACKENZIE, B.A.,

Scholar of Trinity College.

The Christian Clergy of the First Ten Centuries; their Beneficial Influence on European Progress.

Crown 8vo. cloth, 6*s*. 6*d*.

"*He has shown considerable research into the History of the early Clergy, and expresses himself with a facility and force which many an experienced writer may envy. He has displayed in this essay a sound judgment, a freedom from prejudice, and a conscientious endeavour to reach the truth, which convinces us that an able and excellent man was lost to the world by the untimely death of* HENRY MACKENZIE."—ATHENÆUM, Jan. 12, 1856.

"*We rarely meet with a prize-essay of so much general interest.*"
GUARDIAN, Feb. 6, 1856.

BY DAVID MASSON, M.A.,

Professor of English Literature in University College, London.

Essays, Biographical and Critical: chiefly on English Poets.

8vo. cloth, 12*s.* 6*d.*

OPINIONS.

"*Mr. Masson has succeeded in producing a series of criticisms in relation to creative literature, which are satisfactory as well as subtile,—which are not only ingenious, but which possess the rarer recommendation of being usually just . . . But we pass over these Essays to that which is in the main a new, and, according to our judgment, an excellent biographical sketch of Chatterton. . . This 'Story of the Year* 1770,' *as Mr. Masson entitles it, stands for nearly* 200 *pages in his volume, and contains, by preference, the fruits of his judgment and research in an elaborated and discursive memoir. . . Its merit consists in the illustration afforded by Mr. Masson's inquiries into contemporary circumstances, and the clear traces thus obtained of Chatterton's London life and experience. . . . Mr. Masson unravels this mystery very completely.*"—TIMES, Nov. 4, 1856.

"*No one who reads a single page of Mr. Masson will be likely to content himself with that alone. He will see at a glance that he has come across a man endowed with a real love of poetry; a clear, fresh, happy insight into the poet's heart; and a great knowledge of the historical connexion of its more marked epochs in England. He has distinct and pleasant thoughts to utter; he is not above doing his very best to utter them well; there is nothing slovenly or clumsy or untidy in their expression; they leap along in a bright stream, bubbling, sparkling, and transparent.*"—THE GUARDIAN, Nov. 5, 1856.

"*Worthy of being ranked among the very foremost of their class. . . The longest and finest composition of the work—a gem in literary biography—is its 'Chatterton, a Story of the Year* 1770.' . . . *This singularly interesting and powerful biography fills up this sad outline as it never was filled up before.*"
EDINBURGH WITNESS (edited by Hugh Miller), Aug. 23, 1856.

"*His life of Chatterton is a complete, symmetrical and marvellous work of art . . . a classical biography.*"—THE GLASGOW COMMONWEALTH, Aug. 16, 1856.

"*Will secure both attention and respect.*"—EXAMINER, Sept. 6, 1856.

"*Very admirable criticisms, which show not only a thorough acquaintance with the works he criticises, but a deep sense of poetic beauty.*"
DAILY NEWS, Aug. 5, 1856.

"*We know not where to find a larger amount of discriminating, far-seeing, and genial criticism within the same compass.*"
BRITISH QUARTERLY REVIEW, July, 1856.

"*Here is a biography (the essay on Chatterton) told without exaggeration, without unwarranted use of hypothetic incidents, yet surpassing the most highly-wrought fiction in its power over our emotions.*"
THE WESTMINSTER REVIEW, July, 1856.

"*Not only a series of biographical studies, but in some sort a philosophical history of English poetry from Shakspeare to Alexander Smith.*"
THE LEADER, June 4, 1856.

"*Distinguished by a remarkable power of analysis, a clear statement of the actual facts on which speculation is based, and an appropriate beauty of language. These Essays should be popular with serious men.*"
THE ATHENÆUM, May 24, 1856.

BY JOHN HAMILTON, (of St. Ernan's,) M.A.

Of St. John's College, Cambridge.

On Truth and Error: Thoughts, in Prose and Verse, on the Principles of Truth, and the Causes and Effects of Error. Crown 8vo. bound in cloth, with red leaves, 10*s*. 6*d*. *Just ready.*

BY THE REV. F. D. MAURICE, M.A.,

Chaplain of Lincoln's Inn.

1. The Gospel of St. John. A Series of Discourses. Second Edition, Crown 8vo. cloth, 10*s*. 6*d*. *Just ready.*

2. The Doctrine of Sacrifice deduced from the Scriptures. Crown 8vo. cloth, 7*s*. 6*d*.

3. Learning and Working. The Religion of Rome, and its influence on Modern Civilization. In 1 vol. Crown 8vo. cloth, 5*s*.

4. Lectures on the Ecclesiastical History of the First and Second Centuries. 8vo. cloth, 10*s*. 6*d*.

5. Theological Essays. Second Edition. Crown 8vo. 10*s*. 6*d*.

6. Patriarchs and Lawgivers of the Old Testament. Second Edition. Crown 8vo. cloth, 6*s*.

7. Prophets and Kings of the Old Testament. Second Edition. Crown 8vo. cloth, 10*s*. 6*d*.

8. The Unity of the New Testament. Lectures on the Gospels of St. Matthew, St. Mark, and St. Luke, and on the Epistles of St. Paul, St. Peter, St. James, and St. Jude. 8vo. cloth, 14*s*.

REV. F. D. MAURICE'S WORKS—continued.

9. Christmas Day, and other Sermons. 8vo. cloth, 10*s.* 6*d.*

10. On the Religions of the World. Third Edition. Fcp. 8vo. cloth, 5*s.*

CONTENTS: Mahometanism—Hindooism—Buddhism—The Old Persian Faith—The Egyptian—The Greek—The Roman—The Gothic—The Relation between Christianity and Hindooism, &c.

11. On the Prayer-Book. Second Edition. Fcp. 8vo. cloth, 5*s.* 6*d.*

12. The Church a Family. Fcp. 8vo. cloth, 4*s.* 6*d.*

13. On the Lord's Prayer. Third Edition. Fcp. 8vo. cloth, 2*s.* 6*d.*

14. On the Sabbath, and other Sermons. Fcp. 8vo. cloth, 2*s.* 6*d.*

15. Law on the Fable of the Bees. Fcp. 8vo. cloth, 4*s.* 6*d.*

The Word "Eternal" and the Punishment of the Wicked. Third Edition. 1*s.*

Eternal Life and Eternal Death. 1*s.* 6*d.*

The Name Protestant. Three Letters to Mr. Palmer. Second Edition. 3*s.*

Right and Wrong Methods of Supporting Protestantism. 1*s.*

The Duty of a Protestant in the Oxford Election. 1847. 1*s.*

The Case of Queen's College, London. 1*s.* 6*d.*

Plan of a Female College. 6*d.*

Death and Life. In Memoriam C. B. M. 1*s.*

Administrative Reform. 3*d.*

PROSPECTUS OF A SERIES

OF

MANUALS FOR THEOLOGICAL STUDENTS

NOW IN COURSE OF PUBLICATION.

It is now about four years since the Prospectus of this Series was first issued. Four volumes have now been published, and several others are in an advanced state. The reception which the volumes already published have met with, has fully justified the anticipation with which the Publishers commenced the Series, and warrants them in the belief, that their aim of supplying books "concise, comprehensive, and accurate," "convenient for the professional Student and interesting to the general reader," has been not unsuccessfully fulfilled.

The following paragraphs appeared in the original Prospectus, and may bo here conveniently reproduced :—

"The Authors being Clergymen of the English Church, and the Series being designed primarily for the use of Candidates for office in her Ministry, the books will seek to be in accordance with her spirit and principles ; and therefore, (*because* the spirit and principles of the English Church teach charity and truth,) in treating of the opinions and principles of other communions, every effort will be made to avoid acrimony or misrepresentation.

" It will be the aim of the writers throughout the Series to avoid all dogmatic expression of doubtful or individual opinions."

THE FOUR FOLLOWING VOLUMES ARE NOW READY :—

THEOLOGICAL MANUALS—continued.

1. A General View of the History of the Canon of the New Testament during the FIRST FOUR CENTURIES.

Crown 8vo. cloth, 12*s*. 6*d*.

BY BROOKE FOSS WESTCOTT, M.A.,

Assistant Master of Harrow School, formerly Fellow of Trinity College, Cambridge.

OPINIONS OF THE PRESS.

"*A work which forms one of the invaluable series of Theological Manuals now in course of publication at Cambridge.*"
BRITISH AND FOREIGN EVANGELICAL REVIEW, July, 1856.

"*The Author is one of those who are teaching us that it is possible to rifle the storehouses of German theology, without bearing away the taint of their atmosphere: and to recognise the value of their accumulated treasures, and even track the vagaries of their theoretic ingenuity, without abandoning in the pursuit the clear sight and sound feeling of English common sense . . . . It is by far the best and most complete book of the kind; and we should be glad to see it well placed on the lists of our examining chaplains.*"—GUARDIAN, Oct. 3, 1855.

"*Learned, dispassionate, discriminating, worthy of his subject and the present state of Christian Literature in relation to it.*"
BRITISH QUARTERLY, Oct. 3, 1855.

"*To the student in Theology it will prove an admirable Text-Book: and to all others who have any curiosity on the subject it will be satisfactory as one of the most useful and instructive pieces of history which the records of the Church supply.*"—LONDON QUARTERLY, Oct. 1855.

"*The Author carries into the execution of his design a careful and painstaking scholarship . . . . Considered as a list of* Testimonials *in favour of the canonical writings, our Author's work deserves the praise of great diligence and manifest conscientiousness.*"—NATIONAL REVIEW, Oct. 1855.

"*If the rest of the series of manuals, of which the present volume forms a part, are as ably executed, the Christian public will be greatly indebted to the projectors of the plan.*"—LITERARY CHURCHMAN.

"*There is nothing, so far as we know, resembling it in the English tongue . . . We have here presented to us a striking and luminous view of a very broad and comprehensive subject, marked throughout by rich and copious erudition. A volume which we consider a most valuable addition to the literature of Revelation. Scripture Expositors, of whatever name, will acknowledge that they have been laid under deep obligation by the work of* MR. WESTCOTT."
BRITISH BANNER, Jan. 4, 1856.

"*The conception of the work, and the discrimination and learning with which it is executed, adapt it most thoroughly to the present state and forms of controversy on the subject to which it relates.*"—NONCONFORMIST, Jan. 23, 1856.

THEOLOGICAL MANUALS—continued.

2. A History of the Christian Church during the Reformation.

By CHARLES HARDWICK, M.A., Fellow of St. Catharine's College, Cambridge, Divinity Lecturer of King's College, and Christian Advocate in the University of Cambridge.

Crown 8vo. cloth, 10*s*. 6*d*.

OPINIONS OF THE PRESS.

"*The whole volume displays a profusion of learning, great accuracy and honesty in collecting and collating authorities, a clear as well as a concise narrative of events; and it always refers to the authorities on which the history is grounded.*"
CHRISTIAN REMEMBRANCER, April, 1856.

"*Exhibits a deep comprehension and a firm grasp of his theme, with the ease and mastery in treatment which such qualities generally impart.............The utility of* MR. HARDWICK'S *work consists in bringing the greater and minor histories connected with the Reformation into a single volume of compact shape, as well as presenting their broad features to the student. The merit of the history consists in the penetration with which the opinions of the age, the traits of its remarkable men, and the intellectual character of the history, are perceived, and the force with which they are presented.*"—SPECTATOR, March 15, 1856.

"*A more satisfactory manual than England has hitherto produced.........He has laboured learnedly and diligently, at first hand, among the sources and authorities for the ecclesiastical history of the period of which he writes; and has produced a work really original, as far as such a work can be; independent in its judgments; written with taste and feeling; and offering, in its large body of notes, aids and guidance to the fullest investigation the subject can possibly receive.*"—NONCONFORMIST, April 16, 1856.

"*His readers will find him a lively, a luminous, and interesting companion, as well as a generally trustworthy guide.*"—BRITISH BANNER, March 13, 1855.

"*He enters fairly into the questions of which he speaks, and does not attempt to evade their difficulty by vague statements . . . We cordially recommend this work to those who desire an orderly and lucid summary of the leading events of the Reformation . . . We may also observe, that Mr. Hardwick has availed himself of the latest German authorities.*"
LITERARY CHURCHMAN, May 3, 1856.

"*The style is lucid and the plan comprehensive. The facts are well arranged, and their relations ably brought out . . . Will be esteemed by most students as judicious, helpful, and suggestive.*"
EVANGELICAL REVIEW, May, 1856.

"*He writes from genuine and independent sources. Though his work is short, it partakes in no respect of the character of a compilation.*"
THE PRESS, July 12, 1856.

"*It is impossible to speak too highly of the extensive and careful research the book everywhere manifests.*"—BAPTIST MAGAZINE, Aug. 1856.

THEOLOGICAL MANUALS—continued.

3. A History of the Christian Church from the Seventh

Century to the Reformation. By CHARLES HARDWICK, M.A., Fellow of St. Catharine's College, Divinity Lecturer of King's College, and Christian Advocate in the University of Cambridge, Author of "A History of the XXXIX Articles." *With Four Maps constructed for this Work by A. Keith Johnston.*

Crown 8vo. cloth, 10*s.* 6*d.*

OPINIONS OF THE PRESS.

"*It is full in references and authority, systematic and formal in division, with enough of life in the style to counteract the dryness inseparable from its brevity, and exhibiting the results rather than the principles of investigation.* MR. HARDWICK *is to be congratulated on the successful achievement of a difficult task.*"—CHRISTIAN REMEMBRANCER, Oct. 1853.

"*He has bestowed patient and extensive reading on the collection of his materials; he has selected them with judgment; and he presents them in an equable and compact style.*"—SPECTATOR, Sept. 17, 1853.

"*This book is one of a promised series of* 'THEOLOGICAL MANUALS.' *In one respect, it may be taken as a sign of the times. It is a small unpretending volume in appearance, but it is based on learning enough to have sufficed, half a century since, for the ground of two or three quartos, or at least for several portly octavos. For its purpose it is admirable, giving you a careful and intelligent summary of events, and at the same time indicating the best sources of information for the further guidance of the student. Among the authorities thus referred to, we find the most modern as well as the most ancient, the continental as well as the English.*"—BRITISH QUARTERLY, Nov. 1853.

"*It is distinguished by the same diligent research and conscientious acknowledgment of authorities which procured for* MR. HARDWICK'S 'History of the Articles of Religion' *such a favourable reception.*"

NOTES AND QUERIES, Oct. 8, 1853.

"*To a good method and good materials* MR. HARDWICK *adds that great virtue, a perfectly transparent style. We did not expect to find great literary qualities in such a manual, but we* have *found them; we should be satisfied in this respect with conciseness and intelligibility; but while this book has both, it is also elegant, highly finished, and highly interesting.*"

NONCONFORMIST, Nov. 30, 1853.

"*As a manual for the student of Ecclesiastical History in the Middle Ages, we know no English work which can be compared to* MR. HARDWICK'S *book. It has two great merits, that it constantly refers the reader to the authorities, both original and critical, on which its statements are founded; and that it preserves a just proportion in dealing with various subjects.*"

GUARDIAN, April 12, 1854.

THEOLOGICAL MANUALS—continued.

4. A History of the Book of Common Prayer,

together with a Rationale of the several Offices. By the Rev. FRANCIS PROCTER, M.A., Vicar of Witton, Norfolk, formerly Fellow of St. Catharine's College, Cambridge. Second Edition, revised and enlarged. Crown 8vo. cloth, 10*s.* 6*d.*

"MR. PROCTER'S 'History of the Book of Common Prayer' *is by far the best commentary extant . . . . . . Not only do the present illustrations embrace the whole range of original sources indicated by* MR. PALMER, *but* MR. PROCTER *compares the present Book of Common Prayer with the Scotch and American forms; and he frequently sets out in full the Sarum Offices. As a manual of extensive information, historical and ritual, imbued with sound Church principles, we are entirely satisfied with* MR. PROCTER'S *important volume.*"

CHRISTIAN REMEMBRANCER, April, 1855.

"*It is a résumé of all that has been done in the way of investigation in reference to the Prayer-Book.*"—ATHENÆUM, Feb. 17, 1855.

"*We can have little doubt that* MR. PROCTER'S *History of our Liturgy will soon supersede the well-known work of* WHEATLY, *and become a much-used hand-book beyond the circuits of the University for the more immediate use of which it has been produced.*"— NOTES AND QUERIES, March, 1855.

"*Although very decidedly anti-Roman in its tone, we gladly accept it as a substitute for the dull and dreary dogmatism of* WHEATLY. *It presents, in a popular and agreeable narrative, the history of those variations to which so much attention has been directed during the late eventful controversies; and while it contains a very careful, learned and scholarlike exposition of these changes, it also furnishes a most valuable commentary on the successive texts of the formularies themselves, as they are exhibited either in the original editions, or in the useful manuals of* BULLEY *and* KEELING." DUBLIN REVIEW (*Roman Catholic*), April, 1855.

"*We can speak with just praise of this compendious but comprehensive volume. It appears to be compiled with great care and judgment, and has profited largely by the accumulated materials collected by the learning and research of the last fifty years. It is a manual of great value to the student of Ecclesiastical History and of almost equal interest to every admirer of the Liturgy and Services of the English Church.*"—LONDON QUARTERLY REVIEW, April, 1855.

"*It is indeed a complete and fairly-written history of the Liturgy; and from the dispassionate way in which disputed points are touched on, will prove to many troubled consciences what ought to be known to them, viz.:—that they may, without fear of compromising the principles of evangelical truth, give their assent and consent to the contents of the Book of Common Prayer.* MR. PROCTER *has done a great service to the Church by this admirable digest.*"

CHURCH OF ENGLAND QUARTERLY, April, 1855.

FOR A LIST OF THOSE IN IMMEDIATE PREPARATION, SEE NEXT PAGE.

Theological Manuals.

THE FOLLOWING WORKS OF THE SERIES ARE IN PREPARATION.

An Introduction to the Study of the Old Testament, with an Outline of Scripture History.

Notes, Critical and Explanatory, on the Hebrew Text of the Prophet ISAIAH.

The New Testament in the Original Greek: a revised Text.

An Introduction to the Study of the Gospels.
[*In the Press.*

———————————— *Epistles.*

Notes, Critical and Explanatory, on the Greek Text of the FOUR GOSPELS AND THE ACTS OF THE APOSTLES.

Notes, Critical and Explanatory, on the Greek Text of the CANONICAL EPISTLES AND THE APOCALYPSE.

A History of the Christian Church during THE FIRST SIX CENTURIES.

A History of the Christian Church from the Beginning of the XVIIth CENTURY TO THE PRESENT TIME.

An Historical Exposition of the Apostles', Nicene, and *Athanasian* CREEDS.

An Exposition of the Articles of the Church of England.

Others are in progress, and will be announced in due time.

THE JOURNAL OF CLASSICAL AND SACRED PHILOLOGY.

Nos I. to X. price 4*s.* each. Vols I. II. and III. in cloth, 12*s.* 6*d.* each.

This Journal has been established as a medium of communication between Scholars and others interested in Classical and Sacred Philology. The first number appeared in March, 1854; and it is proposed to continue the publication of three numbers, forming a volume yearly, in March, June, and December.

A FEW COMPLETE COPIES IN 9 VOLS. 8VO. CLOTH, PRICE £7 4*s.*, CAN STILL BE HAD OF

THE CAMBRIDGE AND DUBLIN MATHEMATICAL JOURNAL.

WITH AN INDEX OF SUBJECTS AND OF AUTHORS.

This important Work was commenced in 1846, and the last volume was completed in 1854. During these nine years, it received original contributions on almost every branch of pure and applied Mathematics, by many of the most distinguished British Mathematicians, and also by several of the most eminent Foreign. It may, therefore, justly claim a place in every Scientific, Public, or Private Library.

"*Another instance of the efficiency of the course of study in this University, in producing not merely expert algebraists, but sound and original mathematical thinkers, (and, perhaps, a more striking one, from the generality of its contributors being men of comparatively junior standing), is to be found in this Journal, which is full of very original communications.*"—SIR JOHN HERSCHEL'S Address at the British Association.

"*A work of great merit and service to science. Its various contributors have exhibited extensive mathematical learning and vigorous originality of thought.*"—SIR W. ROWAN HAMILTON.

"*A publication which is justly distinguished for the originality and elegance oj its contributions to every department of analysis.*"—REV. PROF. PEACOCK.

MATHEMATICAL CLASS BOOKS
FOR
COLLEGES AND SCHOOLS.

PROFESSOR BOOLE'S TREATISE ON DIFFERENTIAL EQUATIONS. [*Nearly ready.*

MR. COOPER'S GEOMETRICAL CONIC SECTIONS. [*In the Press.*

MR. DREW'S GEOMETRICAL CONIC SECTIONS. [*Immediately.*

MR. FROST'S NEWTON, SECTIONS I. II. III. With Notes and Problems. 10*s.* 6*d.*

MR. GODFRAY'S TREATISE ON THE LUNAR THEORY. 5*s.* 6*d.*

MR. GRANT'S PLANE ASTRONOMY. 6*s.*

MR. HEMMING'S DIFFERENTIAL AND INTEGRAL CALCULUS. Second Edition. 9*s.*

MR. PARKINSON'S ELEMENTARY MECHANICS. 9*s.* 6*d.*

MR. PARKINSON'S ELEMENTARY TREATISE ON OPTICS. [*Preparing.*

MR. PEARSON'S TREATISE ON FINITE DIFFERENCES. Second Edition. 5*s.*

MR. PHEAR'S ELEMENTARY HYDROSTATICS. 5*s.* 6*d.*

MR. PHEAR'S ELEMENTARY MECHANICS. 10*s.* 6*d.*

MR. PUCKLE'S ELEMENTARY CONIC SECTIONS. Second Edition. 7*s.* 6*d.*

MR. BARNARD SMITH'S ARITHMETIC AND ALGEBRA. Fourth Edition. 10*s.* 6*d.*

MR. BARNARD SMITH'S ARITHMETIC FOR SCHOOLS. Fifth Thousand. 4*s.* 6*d.*

MR. BARNARD SMITH'S KEY TO THE ABOVE. 8*s.* 6*d.*

MR. BARNARD SMITH'S MECHANICS AND HYDROSTATICS. [*Preparing.*

MR. SNOWBALL'S PLANE AND SPHERICAL TRIGONOMETRY. Eighth Edition. 7*s.* 6*d.*

MR. SNOWBALL'S INTRODUCTION TO PLANE TRIGONOMETRY. Second Edition. 5*s.*

MR. SNOWBALL'S CAMBRIDGE COURSE OF NATURAL PHILOSOPHY. Fourth Edition. 5*s.*

PROF. TAIT'S AND MR. STEELE'S TREATISE ON DYNAMICS. 10*s.* 6*d.*

MR. TODHUNTER'S TREATISE ON DIFFERENTIAL AND ELEMENTS OF INTEGRAL CALCULUS. Second Edition. 10*s.* 6*d.*

MR. TODHUNTER'S TREATISE ON INTEGRAL CALCULUS AND ITS APPLICATIONS. [*Just ready.* 10*s.* 6*d.*

MATHEMATICAL CLASS BOOKS—continued.

MR. TODHUNTER'S ANALYTICAL STATICS. 10*s.* 6*d.*

MR. TODHUNTER'S CONIC SECTIONS. 10*s.* 6*d.*

MR. TODHUNTER'S TREATISE ON ALGEBRA. [*Preparing.*

MR. TODHUNTER'S ALGEBRA FOR BEGINNERS. [*Preparing.*

PROF. WILSON'S TREATISE ON DYNAMICS. 9*s.* 6*d.*

CAMBRIDGE SENATE-HOUSE PROBLEMS, 1848 TO 1851. With Solutions by Messrs. FERRERS and JACKSON. 15*s.* 6*d.*

CAMBRIDGE SENATE-HOUSE RIDERS, 1848 TO 1851. With Solutions by Mr. JAMESON. 7*s.* 6*d.*

CAMBRIDGE SENATE-HOUSE PROBLEMS, AND RIDERS FOR 1857. With Solutions by the Moderators and Examiners. [*Nearly ready.*

CAMBRIDGE SENATE-HOUSE PROBLEMS AND RIDERS. 1854. With Solutions by the Moderators, Messrs. WALTON & MACKENZIE. 10*s.* 6*d.*

GREEK AND LATIN CLASS BOOKS.

MR. DRAKE'S EUMENIDES OF ÆSCHYLUS. With English Notes. 7*s.* 6*d.*

MR. DRAKE'S DEMOSTHENES DE CORONA. With English Notes. 5*s.*

MR. FROST'S THUCYDIDES, BOOK VI. With English Notes. 7*s.* 6*d.*

DR. HUMPHREYS' EXERCITATIONES IAMBICÆ. Second Edition. 5*s.* 6*d.*

MR. MAYOR'S JUVENAL. With English Notes. 10*s.* 6*d.*

MR. MERIVALE'S SALLUST. With English Notes. 5*s.*

MR. THRING'S CONSTRUING BOOK. 2*s.* 6*d.*

MR. WRIGHT'S HELLENICA. With English Notes. 3*s.* 6*d.*

MR. WRIGHT'S HELP TO LATIN GRAMMAR. 4*s.* 6*d.*

MR. WRIGHT'S THE SEVEN KINGS OF ROME; A FIRST LATIN CONSTRUING BOOK. With English Notes. 3*s.*

MR. WRIGHT'S VOCABULARY AND EXERCISES FOR THE ABOVE. [*Just ready.* 2*s.* 6*d.*

ENGLISH GRAMMARS.

MR. THRING'S ELEMENTS OF GRAMMAR. New Edition. 2*s.*

MR. THRING'S CHILD'S GRAMMAR. New Edition. 1*s.*

MR. PARMINTER'S MATERIALS FOR ENGLISH GRAMMAR. 3*s.* 6*d.*

LATELY PUBLISHED.

MR. SWAINSON'S HANDBOOK TO BUTLER'S ANALOGY. 2*s.*

MR. CROSSE'S ANALYSIS OF PALEY'S EVIDENCES. 3*s.* 6*d.*

MR. SIMPSON'S EPITOME OF CHURCH HISTORY. New Edition. 5*s.*

R. CLAY, PRINTER, BREAD STREET HILL.

www.ingramcontent.com/pod-product-compliance
Lightning Source LLC
LaVergne TN
LVHW011209110826
845150LV00006B/1372